Coast

40 Coast &
Country Walks

The authors and publisher have made every effort to ensure that the information in this publication is accurate, and accept no responsibility whatsoever for any loss, injury or inconvenience experienced by any person or persons whilst using this book.

published by
pocket mountains ltd
The Old Church, Annanside,
Moffat DG10 9HB

ISBN: 978-1-907025-990

Text and photography copyright © Darren Flint and Donald Greig 2023

The right of Darren Flint and Donald Greig to be identified as the Authors of this work has been asserted by them in accordance with the Copyright, Designs and Patents Act 1988

A catalogue record for this book is available from the British Library

Contains Ordnance Survey data © Crown copyright and database 2023 supported by out of copyright mapping 1945-1961

Printed by J Thomson Colour Printers, Glasgow

MIX
Paper | Supporting
responsible forestry
FSC® C023105

Introduction

Although long celebrated for its lakes and mountains, Cumbria's coastline offers as much interest and beauty as the county's interior but receives nothing like the same number of visitors and seldom feels as busy. With its attractions spread out down its length of 160km or so, there's plenty of space for those discerning visitors who make it beyond the fells to this enticing shoreline.

Here, too, are significant population centres – places of past and present industry, such as Workington, Whitehaven and Barrow-in-Furness, interspersed with busy and historic towns at Silloth, Maryport, Egremont, Millom and Ulverston. In summer, the long stretches of shingle and sand that line the Solway Firth in the north are a major draw, while birds wheel above the cliffs of the central coast around St Bees. From the shore around the Furness Peninsula and Kent estuary in the south, the vast expanse of Morecambe Bay stretches beguilingly as far as the eye can see.

History

This is border country, where boundaries in both the north and south have been disputed over centuries and where warring nations have repeatedly come face to face in battles and cross-border raids. Roman Cumbria formed the northwest frontier of Britain and of the Roman Empire, with the construction of Hadrian's Wall at the Tyne-Solway isthmus redefining Roman territory in a retreat from the Antonine Wall further north. Several of the walks in this guide trace sections of this great symbol of Roman power.

In the 10th and 11th centuries, Cumbria bounced between the English, Scots and Northumbrians, with competing factions all vying for control of territory and strategic north-south routes. Come the Normans, William I's conquest stumbled in Cumbria, which by then was a no-man's land between England and Scotland. William II took a firmer hold and built a castle at Carlisle to help shore up the northern defences. Despite this, the Scots held the castle and town to siege no fewer than seven times between 1173 and 1461, making it the most frequently besieged place in the British Isles. Egremont Castle, too, was built around this time, with the town growing up around it. Profits from the local market were almost certainly used in founding St Bees Priory. Carlisle Castle makes for a fitting start point for the first walk in this volume, with both Egremont Castle and St Bees featuring later on.

Despite regular skirmishes, relative peace prevailed for two centuries. The Norman Priory Church in Carlisle became a cathedral in 1133 and abbeys were founded across the region, including those at Holme Cultram (now Abbeytown) and on the Furness Peninsula. Eventually, though, the Wars of Scottish Independence spilled over the border in the 13th and 14th centuries. Edward I (Longshanks, Hammer of the Scots), Robert the Bruce and William Wallace all made their presence felt and, in 1307, camped on the Solway Plain with Scotland tantalisingly in sight, Edward drew his last breath. The spot where he died is marked today with a memorial and is visited on the Burgh by Sands walk.

From the 14th to 17th centuries, there was almost constant unrest due in large part to the Border Reivers, local clans from north and south of the border who regularly raided each other's lands for cattle. The Union of the Crowns in 1603 marked a turning point, when James VI of Scotland acceded to the throne as James I of England, subsequently bringing his unruly northern territories to heel.

The dawn of the Industrial Revolution brought development down the Cumbrian coast, where coal and iron mined since the 17th century in the area around Workington and Whitehaven were used in the developing shipyards at Barrow-in-Furness, transforming what was once a small hamlet into a world-renowned manufacturing centre for submarines (a walk from Barrow to Roa Island sets out through the dockyards). Around the same time, a nascent tourism industry in and around the Cumbrian lakes grew rapidly with the development of local infrastructure, especially the railways, leading eventually to the creation of the Lake District National Park in 1951. Four of the walks in this guide are inside the park, while three others traverse its boundaries.

The Cumbrian Coast today is a fascinating mix of rural and industrial, maritime and mountainous. Arable and livestock farms abut the sandy shores of the Solway and energy producers capitalise on the elements, with both on- and off-shore windfarms and the nuclear power station at Sellafield. For walkers, there is an almost endless choice of superb routes suitable for all abilities.

Walking, weather and safety

Despite being only a short hop from Carlisle and within easy reach of the tourism honeypots of the Lake District National Park, this area remains relatively undiscovered. On many of the walks in this volume, beyond the towns and villages, you might have a beach, estuary or fell all to yourself.

Cumbrian weather is notoriously fickle, especially – but not exclusively – on the higher ground beyond the coastal plain. Snow can linger on the higher ground longer here than in many other parts of the country, spring may arrive later and late frosts are not uncommon.

Seasonal variations mean that the worst excesses of the weather are likely to be avoided in spring and summer and, more often than not, walking on the coast itself is without problem. Indeed, on a sunny day it is positively blissful. But rapidly changing conditions are not uncommon and in the hills, in particular, when the clouds descend and the mists obscure the way ahead, there can be little choice but to rely on a compass or turn back. The advice, therefore, is to be prepared, with layers of clothing, waterproofs, a compass, OS map and something to eat and drink. And if in doubt about conditions or your own ability to navigate, don't be afraid to retreat.

Transport

Travel by train is one of the joys of this area. An impressive 26 stations mark the progress of the Cumbrian Coast Line as it runs from Carlisle all the way down to Barrow-in-Furness. Note that some places are request stations, so check in advance and if need be make your destination known to the guard on boarding.

There are another 11 stations on the Furness Line which runs from Barrow to Lancaster, including Ulverston, Grange-over-Sands and Arnside.

Although a bus network operates down the length of the coast, it mostly serves the main towns, making some of the more rural parts hard to reach. Taxis may be the only option in such places, in which case it is best to arrange any rides home before setting out as mobile coverage can be patchy.

Many routes start from a small village, beside a church, or pull-in area, where

parking considerably is the order of the day. If an event is on and the car park is busy, please look elsewhere for a space. Take care not to block farm gates.

About the guide

Distances range from 3km to 16km and timings are generally a maximum of three to four hours based on walking 3.5km-4km per hour, plus extra time for harder and steeper terrain. Not included in the times are refreshment breaks, wildlife spotting or stop-offs for visiting attractions or shopping.

Details of the relevant OS Explorer map (1:25,000) are given for each walk. The illustrative maps included for each route are designed to be used in conjunction with the listed OS map and it is recommended that you always carry the relevant OS map with you.

Dogs can be taken on all of these walks and, it goes without saying, need to be kept under control and on a lead through fields of livestock, sensitive wildlife habitats or where signs advise.

A note on livestock: this is farming country and on the majority of walks you're likely to come across livestock, usually sheep in the upland areas and cattle on the lower pastures. Always keep dogs under control and avoid taking them into fields during lambing or calving seasons, which generally run March-May, but could start earlier.

River Eden looking
towards Rockcliffe ▶

Cumbria's northern coast is defined in part by the westernmost section of the Solway Plain. The name is something of a misnomer for the area is not entirely flat. An undulating landscape rolls westwards before dropping to the shores of the Solway Firth, where mudflats stretch out towards Scotland when the tide is out. On a calm day it presents a pastoral scene, with fields of cattle grazing on lush beach-fringed pastures. But when the weather turns, the wind gusts up the channel from the Irish Sea and high tides quickly ravage the shore.

A short distance inland lies the county's only city, Carlisle, home to 110,000 souls and a living testimony to the cross-border tug-of-war that has determined so much of its history. Castle and cathedral stand proud and the River Eden, which was once a key feature in lines of defence, snakes its way westwards through areas that have long since been developed.

For walkers there is much here to enjoy – pretty coastal villages, huge skies with dramatic sunsets, some of England's scarcest habitats and wildlife, and areas of solitude and quiet forming a large part of the Solway Coast Area of Outstanding Natural Beauty (solwaycoastaonb.org.uk). Bowness-on-Solway marks the western end of Hadrian's Wall while, from more recent times, no fewer than six airfields between Carlisle and Silloth testify to the area's historic role in the First and Second World Wars. Military history enthusiasts might want to check out the Solway Military Trails (solwaymilitarytrail.co.uk).

Many of the walks pass through habitats of international significance, including large areas of saltmarsh and various sites within the South Solway Mosses National Nature Reserve. This can be a boggy place and the peat can be 10m deep, so watch your step. Keep your eyes and ears open for, among other things, skylark, red squirrel, adder, curlew, snipe, warblers, marsh fritillary and banded demoiselle damselfly.

Carlisle and the Solway Plain

Carlisle to Rockcliffe

Distance 13.5km **Time** 3 hours (one way)
Terrain town path, country tracks and
riverside paths **Map** OS Explorer 315
Access Carlisle's bus and railway stations
are a five-minute walk from the start; no
public transport back from Rockcliffe, so
a lift or taxi is required to return

The River Eden snakes its way westwards
from Carlisle on its final approach to the
Solway, in parts running slow and deep,
elsewhere frothing and riffling as it
pushes its way insistently downstream.
If you fancy an extended walk, combine
it with the following Rockcliffe route for
a full day out.

   The historic landmarks of Carlisle
Cathedral and Castle are both within
easy reach of the start of this walk at Bitts
Park car park in central Carlisle, and are
worth exploring. From the castle, wander
down into Bitts Park car park and up the
right-hand side of the tennis courts to
the river. Go through the underpass at
the Sands Centre then nip up to the road

and cross the river. On the other side,
drop down through the Chinese/Italian
Gardens and continue downstream under
the bridge. Celandine and daffodils line
the way in spring.

   Skirt the edge of the cricket ground and
wander through the woods. Go left at the
end of the path, then at the main road
walk straight on uphill for 500m. Just after
the imposing sandstone Austin Friars
School on the right, take Etterby Road on
the left for just over 500m. Where Stainton
Road turns sharp right, carry on ahead on
a track down the side of a house,
signposted for the River Eden.

   From here on, simply follow the path
along the riverbank for just over 10km.
Ranks of electricity pylons at the start
soon give way to peaceful views across the
fields, while traffic noise is replaced by the
sounds (and sights) of the river. Birdlife is
plentiful; look out for goosander, ducks,
herons, swans and, in spring and summer,
sand martins darting above the water.
You might even spot an otter.

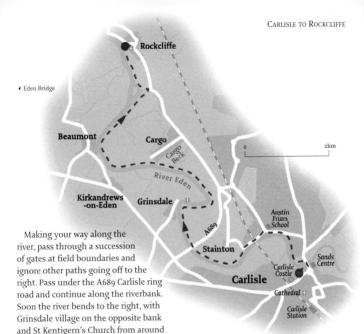

◄ Eden Bridge

Rockcliffe

Beaumont

Cargo

Cargo Beck

River Eden

Kirkandrews -on-Eden

Grinsdale

Austin Friars School

A689

Stainton

Sands Centre

Carlisle Castle

Carlisle

Cathedral ✝

Carlisle Station

0   2km

Making your way along the river, pass through a succession of gates at field boundaries and ignore other paths going off to the right. Pass under the A689 Carlisle ring road and continue along the riverbank. Soon the river bends to the right, with Grinsdale village on the opposite bank and St Kentigern's Church from around 1740 visible high above the water.

As the river bends to the left, stick to the waterside path and climb the short but steep hill. Once over the stile at the top, continue ahead above the river, with views northwards to the distant hills of Dumfries and Galloway. Dropping back down to the river, cross the bridge over Cargo Beck and take the left-hand path along the bank. This is a particularly appealing stretch which is quiet and warm on a sunny day, and a good spot to pause for a picnic with one or two benches dotted along the bank.

Ahead on the opposite bank, the houses at Beaumont come into view. Follow the river as it bends to the right, soon reaching a junction with a byroad from the nearby village of Cargo. Continue ahead but, shortly after, start veering away from the bank to cross a succession of bridges over a number of channels. After the third and fourth bridges, head left. Keep to the riverside path but nip over a stile into the field where the shore runs out.

Ahead, the village of Rockcliffe can be seen. Keep on downstream and, just past the cricket pitch, go right to the church, then right again up the lane, before dropping down to the right for refreshments at the village pub.

9

Rockcliffe

Distance 5km **Time** 1 hour 30
Terrain country lanes, riverside path
Map OS Explorer 303 **Access** no public
transport to the start

Idyllic Rockcliffe with its popular pub
and riverside setting provides an
irresistible focus for this gentle amble
around the village and down country
lanes before skirting the edge of
estuarine Rockcliffe Marsh and returning
along the banks of the Eden. Be aware
that the riverside sections can flood.

Looking at today's peaceable village, it's
hard to imagine that it once played a role
in border skirmishes between England
and Scotland, or that in the 18th century
it was a commercial port and shipbuilding
centre. Starting at St Mary's Church,
where there is limited parking (please

park responsibly), follow the lane down
its left-hand side and continue ahead,
with the open grassy area and river to
your left. A couple of picnic benches here
make a good spot for lingering, with
superb views along the river to
Castletown House. Anthony Turner's
sculpture *Global Warming* stands on its
own, resembling Planet Earth held
carefully in a hand.

Follow the lane uphill and past a
number of houses on a stretch above the
river with glimpses through the trees of
the water below. Stay on the lane where
it bends sharply right and, on reaching
a road, go left for around 200m.

Where the road bends sharply to the
right, with a lodge and entrance to
Castletown Estate on the left, continue
straight ahead, signposted for Rockcliffe

Cross and Wether Hill. Listen out for woodpeckers here in the estate woods. After around 750m, take the lane to the left signposted for Demesne, keeping an eye open for orange-tip butterflies nectaring on pink cuckooflower in spring.

The surrounding land here is part of the Castletown Estate, a 5000-acre farm between the Rivers Esk and Eden which has been home to the Mounsey family since 1802. In addition to producing beef, it is also known for its Rockcliffe saltmarsh lamb. Sea aster, sorrel, sea lavender, milkwort and thrift growing on the marsh provide a distinctive diet for grazing stock.

After roughly 1km, the lane peters out in a farmyard next to Castletown House. Follow the waymarked route straight on over a stile, through a gate and out to the raised embankment path above the river.

A short walk to the right for around 200m leads out to the riverbank, with good views back along to Rockcliffe. Retrace your steps and continue along the raised path which shortly drops down to the riverside. Follow the river and, where the level bank runs out, go over a stile and uphill to reach the lane above the river from your outward route.

Retrace your steps to Rockcliffe and once back at the top of the lane by the church, take the signposted public footpath to the right downhill between the houses to reach the village pub.

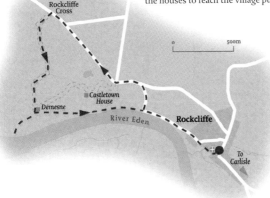

◄ The River Eden with Castletown House beyond

Burgh by Sands

Distance 13km **Time** 3 hours
Terrain country lanes, field and riverside
path, farm track **Map** OS Explorer 315
Access infrequent bus to Burgh by Sands
from Carlisle (except Sundays)

This delightful ramble around Hadrian's
Wall country is replete with interest,
from history to scenic riverside walking.
Traversing sections of both the Cumbrian
Coastal Way and Hadrian's Wall Path, it's
also well signposted and easy to follow.
Note that some sections can flood when
the river is in spate and may become
impassable, with no alternative routes.

Start at the car park at Burgh by Sands,
near the Greyhound Inn. Leaving the car
park, turn right through the village and
then left up the lane which is signposted
for the Edward I Monument. After around
1km, where the road bends sharp right,
bear left on a track and, where it splits
immediately after, take the right fork.
Ahead, views down to the Eden estuary

and the Solway soon open up. The
saltmarshes have been grazed by livestock
since the settlement of Cistercian monks
in 1150AD and the resulting sward is ideal
for migratory birds: swans, geese and
ducks overwinter here. It's also a good
breeding area for ground-nesting birds.

Cross a couple of stiles in quick
succession and then head out to the
monument. It was here in 1307 that
Edward I died of dysentery during one of
his many campaigns against Scotland.

To stick to the right of way, return to the
stile and then go left up the fenceline,
following it all the way out to the
riverbank at Old Sandsfield. Turn east
here along the riverbank in front of the
farmhouse. At New Sandsfield, take the
lane to the right, pass between the
Holmesmill farm buildings and at a
junction go left. After just over 500m,
where the road bends sharp right, take the
left turn. At the next sharp turn in the
road, nip through a kissing gate and head

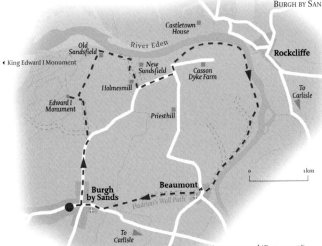

Castletown House

River Eden

Old Sandsfield

New Sandsfield

Rockcliffe

◀ King Edward I Monument

Casson Dyke Farm

To Carlisle

Holmesmill

Edward I Monument

Priesthill

0   1km

Beaumont

Burgh by Sands

Hadrian's Wall Path

To Carlisle

diagonally right out towards the riverbank, crossing over a couple of waymarked bridges en-route.

This is a lovely riverside section of around 3km. On the opposite bank stands Castletown House, just after which note the red escarpment, called Red Rocks. Designated a Regionally Important Geological Site, it was laid down as desert dunes around 300 million years ago. The church spire at Rockcliffe, also on the opposite bank, beckons you on.

Beyond Rockcliffe, keep to the riverbank but follow waymarkers to help navigate the inlets via a couple of bridges. Where the riverbank begins to narrow, head over to the right to take a farm track that climbs the hill (the riverside path is virtually impassable in places beyond here). Stay on the track and on reaching a surfaced lane continue ahead into

Beaumont (pronounced 'Bee-mont'), with a church and a mix of houses clustered around the small green. The church is usually open, so pop in for a moment of peace in what is a simple interior of whitewashed walls and a striking 15th-century roof.

Back at the village green, looking at the church, go right and as you start to head downhill, take the signposted lane to the left. This section of around 1.5km runs in an almost dead straight line between and across fields, emerging onto the road back into Burgh, at which go right. Back in the village, it's worth a stop at St Michael's Church, built on the site of the Roman fort of Aballava and with its quirky granite timeline through the churchyard. It was here that the body of Edward I lay in state.

Exiting the churchyard, continue through the village to return to the start.

Finglandrigg Wood

Distance 3km **Time** 1 hour
Terrain footpath, tracks and boardwalk
Map OS Explorer 314 **Access** infrequent
bus to Finglandrigg Wood NNR (request
stop) from Carlisle

**This gentle saunter takes you through
one of the largest areas of semi-natural
woodland on the Solway Plain with
plenty of wildlife-spotting opportunities.
Note, livestock graze on the reserve.**

If driving, start from the roadside lay-by
on the B5307 between Kirkbampton and
Kirkbride and enter this delightful, pint-
sized National Nature Reserve via the
track by the picnic benches and bike racks.
Finglandrigg Wood's rich mosaic of
habitats – including woodland, peat bog,
heathland and rough pasture – means
there's a chance of spotting red squirrel,
roe deer, common lizard, adder, marsh
fritillary butterfly and up to 40 species of
resident and migratory birds – so keep
your eyes peeled. Walk away from the road
along the surfaced track which is lined
with a vast array of broadleaf trees,
including hawthorn, rowan and oak, all
skirted with a tangle of ferns, rambling
brambles and honeysuckle.

At the obvious fork in the path go
right, heading deeper into the wood,
crossing a stream and keeping to a
boardwalk. Follow the red waymarker
arrows through the woodland, eventually
leaving the trees through a gate onto a
grassland area where cattle are used to
manage this increasingly rare habitat.

In May and June, keep an eye open for
the rare marsh fritillary butterfly with its
brown and orange speckled wings. Once

◄ Boardwalk in Finglandrigg Wood

extinct in England, it now has a foothold here thanks to a successful reintroduction programme which was started back in 2007 at Finglandrigg.

Go through the next gate and follow the long boardwalk running around the edge of Little Bampton Common, a delightful heathland of heather with a peppering of Scots pine and gorse. Common lizard dart along the boardwalk and on warm days between April and September you might even spot a basking adder – although it's more usual for them to slither off at the first vibration.

Leave the boardwalk and carry on through the gate to an area of rough pasture. Between May and July, this is a great location for northern marsh and common spotted orchids. Summer days also bring speckled wood and wall butterflies along the warm woodland edges. Continue through a small area of woodland, looking out for tawny owls and their long nestbox, before pausing on the well-placed bench to soak it all up.

The path now rejoins the outbound route, so turn right and follow this back to the start. For a slightly different return route, take the right-hand option where the path forks.

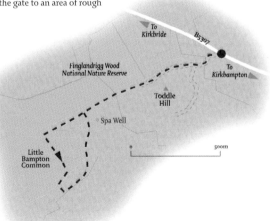

Drumburgh Moss and Glasson

Distance **11.5km** Time **3 hours**
Terrain **footpaths, tracks and quiet lanes**
Map **OS Explorer 314** Access **infrequent
bus from Carlisle to Drumburgh, 1km
from the start**

**Drumburgh Moss Nature Reserve is a joy
to walk at any time of the year, but the
area truly sparkles on sunny days in
spring and summer. Take your time to
explore this watery wonderland awash
with rare plants, birds and reptiles.**

From the Drumburgh Moss parking
area, head back down the access track,
over the cattle grid and go immediately
left to follow the route of Hadrian's Wall
Path. The track meanders across a pretty
pastoral landscape, emerging onto a lane
at the edge of Glasson. This is really the
only section of the walk on which you
might meet other walkers in any number.
You could easily complete the rest of the
route without seeing another soul.

This circular walk heads left along the

lane away from Glasson, but before that
it's worth taking a short detour right,
down through the village, straight over
the coast road and along the footpath to
Raven Bank. This is a pleasant spot to
pause and enjoy the ever-changing Solway
tides and views over to Scotland. When
ready, retrace your steps.

Follow the long straight lane out of
Glasson, imagining how this route would
have once been a simple drover's route
laid on bundles of wood across the boggy
mire. Carry on past Low Flow and the
entrance to Glasson Moss (one for
another day), with views of the Cumbrian
Northern Fells.

Go left at the T-junction, left at the next
junction for Whitrigglees and left again at
the lovely old Cumberland County
Council roadsign. The wide-open views all
around give a real sense of isolation at the
heart of these Solway Plains.

After about 1km, take the footpath on
the left (Cumbria Coastal Way fingerpost)

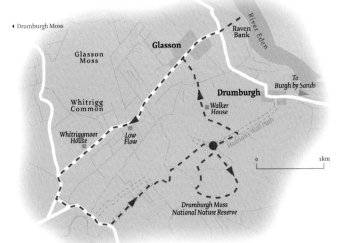

◄ Drumburgh Moss

River Eden

Raven Bank

Glasson

Glasson Moss

Drumburgh

To Burgh by Sands

Walker House

Whitrigg Common

Hadrian's Wall Path

Whitriggmoor House

Low Flow

0   1km

Drumburgh Moss National Nature Reserve

and follow the straight hedge-lined track. Where the track bends sharply left, continue ahead into the nature reserve. Note that at any point on the reserve you might encounter livestock and ponies used for conservation grazing. They are not generally interested in walkers, but give them plenty of space and keep any dogs on a lead.

The rough path winds initially through woodland, then a more open area. At the grazing information boards, cross the stile and follow the tree-lined track left. Climb over another stile onto the broad track crossing the open moss, which soon returns to the parking area. On warm days look out for adders basking in the sun.

Before leaving, take the circular walk around the National Nature Reserve to really experience these wild and unique boggy mires. Take the path by the information shelter, go through the gate and follow the raised paths and boardwalks through the watery pools and boggy areas of spongy sphagnum moss and heather to the raised viewing platform. The mires came into being after the last ice age, when dead vegetation accumulated in areas of standing water to form peat, now one of Western Europe's most threatened habitats. Throughout the year, there is much to see, including white bobbing cotton-grass heads and breeding bird displays in spring, common lizard on the boardwalk and the rare large heath butterfly in summer, peregrine falcon and short-eared owl hunting over the moss in autumn and wildfowl, from the Solway, in winter.

Continue on the path loop exiting through the gate. Turn right, past the bird hide, and carry on back to the car park.

Port Carlisle and Bowness-on-Solway

Distance **6km** Time **1 hour 30**
Terrain **paved road, farm track, fields**
Map **OS Explorer 314** Access **infrequent
bus to Port Carlisle from Carlisle**

**Port Carlisle's port and railway have long
since gone, as has the canal that once
connected it to Carlisle, but with a string
of houses looking out over the shoreside
bowling green to the Solway and Scotland
beyond, its appeal is undiminished.**

Facing the water, go left along the road
from Port Carlisle towards neighbouring
Bowness-on-Solway. Where the Hadrian's
Wall Path joins from the right, keep
straight on. The path itself follows the
road at this point, but there are one or two
spots where it's possible to walk down to
the water's edge to observe the coastal
birds on the mudflats and listen to the
skylarks in the marsh. As with so much of

this coast, the views to Scotland are
expansive: look for the distinctive bulk
of flat-topped Burnswark Hill in the
distance across the water.

Where the road narrows slightly and
starts to corner, drop down to the beach
and continue straight on, shortly reaching
pretty Bowness-on-Solway and a
noticeboard with tidal information.

Rejoin the road and continue into the
village. On reaching the Wesleyan Home
Mission Chapel building of 1872 on the left
(look for the carvings above the door; now
private accommodation), detour to the
right down a path between houses to reach
the Banks. Once popular with the
Edwardians as a place to promenade, it's
now the official start/end of the Hadrian's
Wall Path. Pause a moment in the wooden
pergola to take in the views and the
Roman-style mosaic floor, and to peruse

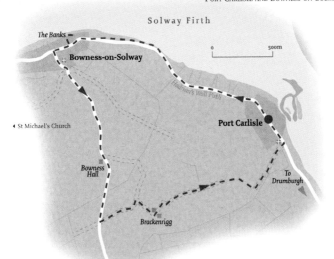

the information boards covering everything from the Roman fort that once occupied the site of the village to Solway birds, Border Reivers, haaf net fishing and more besides.

Continue ahead through the pergola and follow the path back to the main road, where you go right. After passing the Kings Arms pub, take the road to the left, signed for Kirkbride and Wigton. A short distance up the road stands the Norman Church of St Michael, built from stone from Hadrian's Wall. In 1626 its bells were stolen by Border Reivers who crossed the Solway from Scotland. Today it's customary for new vicars to demand their return.

Keep straight on to leave the village and follow the road southwards. Shortly after passing Bowness Hall on the right, head up the Brackenrigg driveway on the left.

Climbing a slight rise, views open up northwards along the Solway and south to the mountains of the Lake District.

Pass in front of Brackenrigg farmhouse and then go immediately left along a waymarked track between the house and the farm sheds. Where the track ends at two gates, continue ahead over a stile and down the field, with the hedgerow on your right. Cross the stile at the bottom of the field and carry on ahead, with the hedgerow on your left. At the end of this field, cross another stile by a metal gate and follow the narrow path lined with hawthorns, a mass of blossom in spring.

Go through the next metal gate and down the side of the Solway Methodist Church building, then turn left along the road to head back into Port Carlisle.

Bowness and Campfield Marsh

Distance 11.5km **Time** 2 hours 30
Terrain footpaths (can be boggy), fields
and quiet lanes **Map** OS Explorer 314
Access infrequent bus to Bowness-on-
Solway from Carlisle

**With Roman history, fine Solway views
and a plethora of nature-rich boggy
mires, this wander around the attractive
village of Bowness-on-Solway and the
nearby common packs in plenty of
interest. Conditions may be squelchy
underfoot, so be sure to wear decent
boots and keep to the paths.**

Standing on the site of a Roman fort
called Maia, Bowness-on-Solway
commands a fine position overlooking
the Solway Firth. From the car park on the
edge of Bowness, head uphill enjoying the
narrow lanes and pretty stone cottages,
then turn right by the Kings Arms pub.
Pause to read the information board
before continuing to St Michael's Church,
built using stone from Hadrian's Wall.

During the more unsettled 'Border
Reiving' times of the 17th century, the
church bells were stolen and accidentally
dropped into the Solway. In retaliation,
bells were stolen from across the water in
Scotland. To this day the communities on
opposite sides of the Solway re-enact
these watery raids.

Carry on along the gorse- and
hawthorn-lined lane for about 2km,
passing through a delightful pastoral
scene. Keep an eye open for scarce tree
sparrows (daintier than their 'house'
cousins, and the males have a chestnut
cap). Ignoring the first footpath on the
right by the entrance to Brackenrigg on
the left, continue to the second, indicated
with a stile into a pasture field (the
fingerpost has long since fallen over).

Cross the field and, at the fence by the
wood, walk around to the left, climb over
another stile and carry on into Bowness
Common. This is the most complete
lowland raised mire in England, a boggy

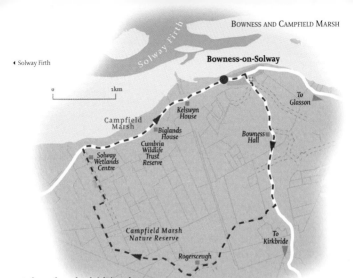

Bowness-on-Solway

◄ Solway Firth

Solway Firth

0   1km

Campfield Marsh

Kelswyn House

Biglands House

Cumbria Wildlife Trust Reserve

Solway Wetlands Centre

Bowness Hall

To Glasson

Campfield Marsh Nature Reserve

Rogersceugh

To Kirkbride

waterlogged peatland rich in sphagnum moss, cotton-grasses and sundews. Look out for more than 100 species of spider, large heath butterfly, curlew and snipe, and, if really lucky, some of the more secretive species such as adder.

Follow the springy path across the heather-clad peatland. The route is marked with poles, but care should be taken not to stray in poor visibility. The path leaves the peatlands over a stile and continues up onto the slightly higher ground of Rogersceugh. Go through the gate, turn right and carry on down to the barn with its various information panels and fine views over the common.

Continue along the track and, where it bends sharply left, go into the field. Take the permissive path downhill, soon joining a boardwalk. There's a well-placed bench where you can enjoy views across

the moss to the masts of RNAS Anthorn and the hills of Galloway beyond.

Where the boardwalk heads sharp right, by the timber compass, take the rough path instead, marked with a red arrow. Soon becoming a boardwalk, carry on along the red route at the fingerpost, which passes through a small woodland of silver birch trees and then runs along the wetlands of RSPB Campfield Marsh Nature Reserve. Lapwing, shelduck and teal are some of the birds to look out for here. On reaching the bird hide, turn left and follow the long straight track up to the Solway Wetlands Centre.

At the road turn right and continue along the Solway back to the start. Be sure to pop into the Cumbria Wildlife Trust Reserve to see if you can spot the rare and elusive willow tit.

Kirkbride

Distance **6km** Time **1 hour 30**
Terrain **footpaths, tracks, fields and
pavement** Map **OS Explorer 314**
Access **infrequent bus to Kirkbride
from Carlisle**

Kirkbride sits on a slight rise in a curve
of the winding River Wampool, just east
of where it empties into the Solway Firth.
This short walk explores the village and
surrounding countryside, a place with a
varied history spanning the centuries
from the Romans to 12th-century monks
and a Second World War airfield.

From the playpark in the centre of the
village, take the no-through road running
along its lower side, past the community
garden to join the main village road. Cross
over, pass The Bush Inn and take Church
Road up to the delightful 12th-century
St Bride's Church. The stone in its
construction is thought to have come
from the nearby Roman fort while the

lane opposite, known locally as the
Wine Lonning, is thought to have been
used by smugglers to carry contraband
from Scotland to the local inns. Due to its
isolated location, St Bride's was once a
target for body snatchers.

Follow the lane around the back of the
church and along the footpath to soon
join a farm track. When this bends sharply
right, go through the kissing gate and
follow the path through a tunnel of trees.
At the end turn left along the grassy track,
a good sheltered spot for butterflies on
warmer days. On reaching the road turn
right, then take a quick left onto another
tree-lined footpath.

Go through the kissing gate and keep to
the field edge, enjoying the fine views
ahead of the Northern Fells and Skiddaw.
Fields around here may look different to
others along the route as they are used for
high-quality turf cutting. Turf from this
area is said to have been used in the

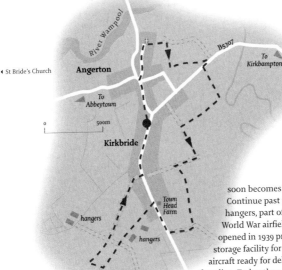

◀ St Bride's Church

Angerton

River Wampool

To
Abbeytown

To
Kirkbampton

BS307

0 ——— 500m

Kirkbride

Town
Head
Farm

hangers

hangers

soon becomes a track. Continue past the large hangers, part of the Second World War airfield that was opened in 1939 primarily as a storage facility for newly-built aircraft ready for delivery to the frontline. Today, the runways are still used by light aircraft while the hangers are used for agricultural storage.

Cross the tarmac drive and follow the fenceline for a short stretch before rejoining the hedge-lined path, which soon curves to the right. Go through a rickety gate and along the barbed-wire fence. Much of this area was impassable marsh until enterprising monks from Melrose Abbey in the Scottish Borders founded nearby Holme Cultram Abbey in the 12th century and set about draining the land. Go through a second gate and, by the bench, take the right fork in the path. Passing the Second World War pillbox, cross the tarmac drive again and continue along the track back to the main street in the village, turning left here to return to the start.

original Wembley Stadium. Continue along the line of the hedge as it turns a sharp right around the field before emerging onto a hedge-lined path.

At the path crossroads, just after the sewage works and bench, turn left to follow the field edge (it can be boggy here after wet weather). Turn right onto the track heading towards the farm buildings, then left along the next hedge (again it may be boggy) and carry on through the kissing gate along the hedge-lined track. At the hard-surfaced track, go straight over and take the track with the stile in the direction of the two aircraft hangers.

On reaching the road, turn right back into Kirkbride and just after Town Head Farm take the lane on the left, which

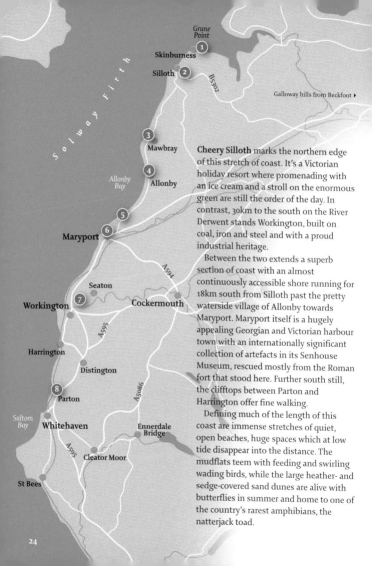

Galloway hills from Beckfoot ▸

Cheery Silloth marks the northern edge of this stretch of coast. It's a Victorian holiday resort where promenading with an ice cream and a stroll on the enormous green are still the order of the day. In contrast, 30km to the south on the River Derwent stands Workington, built on coal, iron and steel and with a proud industrial heritage.

Between the two extends a superb section of coast with an almost continuously accessible shore running for 18km south from Silloth past the pretty waterside village of Allonby towards Maryport. Maryport itself is a hugely appealing Georgian and Victorian harbour town with an internationally significant collection of artefacts in its Senhouse Museum, rescued mostly from the Roman fort that stood here. Further south still, the clifftops between Parton and Harrington offer fine walking.

Defining much of the length of this coast are immense stretches of quiet, open beaches, huge spaces which at low tide disappear into the distance. The mudflats teem with feeding and swirling wading birds, while the large heather- and sedge-covered sand dunes are alive with butterflies in summer and home to one of the country's rarest amphibians, the natterjack toad.

Silloth to Parton

Skinburness and Grune Point

Distance 4.5km **Time** 1 hour
Terrain footpaths, shingle beach and
quiet lanes **Map** OS Explorer 314
Access no public transport to the start

Once an extensive medieval anchorage
and borough, much of Skinburness
was washed away by the sea in the early
14th century. The highlight of this walk
is the windswept Grune Point and the
surrounding mudflats, with far-reaching
views and year-round birdwatching.
For a longer walk, combine it with the
Silloth route via the waterfront path.

  For more than 130 years the Skinburness
Hotel stood on the site of what is now the
parking area in the centre of the village.
Although something of a local landmark,
it was known more for its hardships than
its hospitality: in the course of its history
it bankrupted six owners before two failed
attempts to restore it in the early 2000s
were followed by demolition.

  Turning right out of the parking area,
follow the road around the bend and then
right onto Dick Trod Lane. At the end,
take the coastal path to the right, passing
Chichester Hall retirement home which
was once the elegant residence of a local
cottonmill owner.

  From here, the walk simply loops
around Grune Point, initially following
the Solway Firth before turning inland
to head back to Skinburness along the
saltmarshes. Follow the path around
the back of a beach strewn with white
boulders, up onto a grassy bank past the
lone house, before walking along the
back of a second beach. Just after the
remnants of a concrete structure, head
up the back of the gently shelving beach
to join a well-trodden footpath over the
grassland and past hawthorn trees
distinctly sculpted by the wind.

  The path meanders along the grassland,
following a fenceline for part of the way,

◀ Skinburness

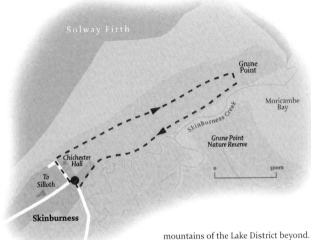

Solway Firth

Grune
Point

Moricambe
Bay

Skinburness Creek

Grune Point
Nature Reserve

0   500m

Chichester
Hall

To
Silloth

Skinburness

through an area great for birdlife. Listen
out for the melodic song of the many
skylarks, particularly in spring and
summer, although they might also be
heard on a sunny winter's day. Keep a look
out too for linnet, stonechat and
whitethroat. Straight ahead on the skyline
stand the prominent masts of RNAS
Anthorn, used for NATO submarine
communications and for transmitting
Greenwich Mean Time – commonly heard
as the 'pips' on the radio.

At the Second World War pillbox, it's
worth lingering for views out over
Moricambe Bay, the saltmarshes and the
mountains of the Lake District beyond.
A good birdwatching spot at any time,
it comes into its own when the tide is
out and the mudflats are transformed
into a giant buffet table for feeding
shelduck, oystercatcher, curlew and many
species of wader.

Turning right at the pillbox, head back
to Skinburness along the edge of the
marshes, which in spring and summer are
a mass of stunning pink thrift flowers.
The path is initially faint on the mud and
shingle shoreline but soon broadens into
a distinct track and eventually an
unmetalled lane lined with pretty
cottages. At the road turn right and head
back to the start.

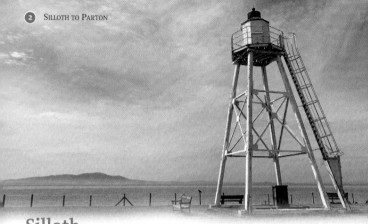

Silloth

Distance 6.5km **Time** 1 hour 30
Terrain pavement, tracks and beach
Map OS Explorer 314 **Access** buses to
Silloth from Maryport and Carlisle

With its extensive green and cobbled
streets lined by attractive buildings,
Silloth wears its Victorian heritage
proudly. It feels a charmingly old-
fashioned sort of place and its appeal
is undeniable. This short loop takes in
its main sights, including a section of
the lengthy promenade, working port
and part of its vast beach.

The Solway Coast Discovery Centre
makes a fitting starting point to this
largely maritime walk and offers
interesting insights into the Solway Coast
Area of Outstanding Natural Beauty
(AONB). On exiting the centre, turn right,
taking the path by the primary school and
down to the cobbled road. Go right again
and follow the seafront along to the white

timber East Cote Lighthouse, built in
1841 as a navigational aid for shipping
between Annan across the water in
Dumfriesshire and Port Carlisle.

For a longer route, continue along the
waterfront to link into the Skinburness
and Grune Point walk, otherwise wander
back a short way to join the promenade
back to Silloth. The town's name
originated from *Sea-lath*, meaning 'The
Barn by the Sea', which was originally part
of a farm belonging to the monks of
nearby Holme Cultram Abbey.

Pass the eye-catching metal sculpture of
the man and his dog on a bench enjoying
the view to Criffel, the dominant hill on
the other side of the water. Just after the
amusement arcade climb the small hill
covered in Scots pine to the Victorian
Pagoda. Built in the 1860s, it commands
fine views. Drop back to the promenade
and, at the RNLI station, turn left.

Modern Silloth grew with the arrival of

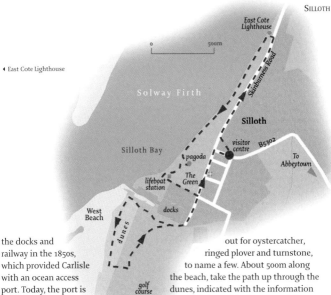

◀ East Cote Lighthouse

the docks and railway in the 1850s, which provided Carlisle with an ocean access port. Today, the port is owned mostly by biscuit manufacturer, Carrs, whose flour mill on a waterside site in the centre of town is still in operation. This is where Jonathan Carr first started milling flour in 1936 for his famous Table Water crackers.

Walk on past The Green and a fine row of terraced houses, before turning right at the crossroads to wander around the back of the port and down to West Beach. Enjoy the vast expanse of beach and mudflats at low water, but keep an eye on the tides. Lonely Lees Scar Lighthouse, built in 1841, stands on a shallow outcrop of hard clay and was manned until 1938. Vast numbers of year-round and migrating birds enjoy the bounty of these ever-changing tides; look out for oystercatcher, ringed plover and turnstone, to name a few. About 500m along the beach, take the path up through the dunes, indicated with the information panel all about this Site of Special Scientific Interest (SSSI), to the edge of the golf course. Turn left onto the track, passing the care home, and once back at the port turn right to return to the town centre.

On reaching the crossroads, you can either explore the buildings, cafés and shops on cobbled Eden and Criffel Streets, or spend time on and around The Green with its well-tended community garden and beds. Either way, pay a visit to the model Lockheed Hudson Bomber plane, an American-built bomber flown mainly by the RAF during the Second World War out of Silloth Airfield.

Finally, turn right onto Petteril Street to return to the start.

29

Mawbray

Distance 4km **Time** 1 hour **Terrain** dunes, footpaths, fields and quiet lanes
Map OS Explorer OL4 **Access** buses to Mawbray from Maryport and Carlisle

With some of the finest sand dunes on the Solway coast, the mysterious rasping of toads each spring and a carpet of purple heather in late summer, there's plenty to discover on this delightfully varied shorter route – whatever the season. Note, cattle graze within the nature reserve and on surrounding farmland.

From the Mawbray Banks Nature Reserve car park, enter the nature reserve through the gate and wend your way along the network of paths criss-crossing the dunes, heath and grasslands. One particularly pleasant route is to keep to the left-hand paths through the dunes, soon coming upon a number of freshwater ponds, home to the UK's loudest amphibian, and one of the rarest too, the natterjack toad. Now restricted almost exclusively to sand dunes around the coast (a single colony has also been found on a Cumbrian fell), the males gather around the breeding pools on warm, still spring nights and emit a loud rasping call, which can be heard up to a mile away. If you're here too late in the year for the calling, the tadpoles can be seen in the pools in May or June, with the toadlets emerging soon after.

Continue through the dunes, enjoying the views over the Solway to Criffel (the big hill on the Scottish side of the Solway), and carry on to the next car park, at which turn right to follow the track up

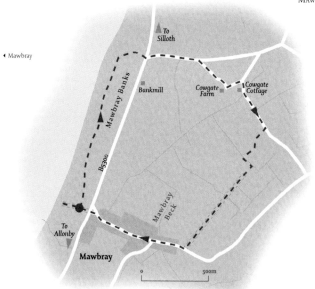

◄ Mawbray

To
Silloth

Mawbray Banks

Bankmill

Cowgate
Farm

Cowgate
Cottage

B5300

Mawbray
Beck

To
Allonby

Mawbray

0   500m

to the road. Carefully cross straight over onto the quiet lane (signed Newton 1), lined with a hedgerow of hawthorn and dog rose, verge-side flowers such as red campion and with views of Cumbria's northern fells. Take the lane to the right, go around the sharp bend at Cowgate Farm and, at the next road junction, turn right again.

Passing Cowgate Cottage, follow the straight lane for about 400m, then take the bridleway on the right signed for Mawbray Road. This field sometimes has grazing cattle in it. Cross the field to the far side, go through the gate, turn left, pass through another gate and then turn right to follow the line of the hedge.

Go through a third gate onto a broad grassy track lined with hedgerow on both sides and a real sense of space and big skies – this is wide open grazing country.

The track joins a lane, at which turn right to follow it into pretty Mawbray village. The community-owned Lowther Arms pub is worth a pitstop. It's dog friendly and has a pleasant beer garden.

Continue along the main street through the village. Back at the coast road, cross straight over and wander back to the car park. It's worth heading down to the beach to see the ever-changing tides. This is a great habitat for wading birds, including oystercatcher, curlew and dainty ringed plover.

Allonby to Crosscanonby

Distance 11.5km **Time** 3 hours (return)
Terrain lanes and woods, with a
sustained climb **Map** OS Explorer OL4
Access no public transport to the start

**The combined footpath and cycleway
along the coast from Allonby offers a
chance for a brisk walk on an accessible
surface with Solway views all the way.**

Directions for this walk are simple.
From Allonby, head south, sticking to the
shorefront and roadside footpath all the
way. If you fancy a change, drop down to
the beach for a bit and linger a while to
gaze across the water to Criffel, the hill
that dominates the skyline on the
Scottish side of the Solway. There's also a
possible teastop after roughly 3km at the
Moody Cow café at Blue Dial Farm.

Take the Crosscanonby turning
and after around 100m head into

Crosscanonby Carr Nature Reserve.
Carr comes from the Norse *Kjar*, meaning
'marsh where willow and alder thrive'.
Vikings settled peacefully in the area
around 1000 years ago. The reserve is a
mix of ponds, meadows and woodland
and is home to a high density of bank
voles, as well as frogs, toads, insects and a
range of birds, including sedge warbler
and reed bunting. A bench and a couple of
tables offer a pleasant spot for a picnic.

Leaving the reserve, go left back towards
the main road, then right at the path
signposted for Salt Pans and Roman Mile
Fortlet 21. Follow the path uphill to the
Roman Fortlet, the only example along
the entire length of Hadrian's Wall to have
been fully uncovered. A clearly discernible
outline gives a good impression of
its size and structure. The apparent
anomaly is that the fortlet was built a

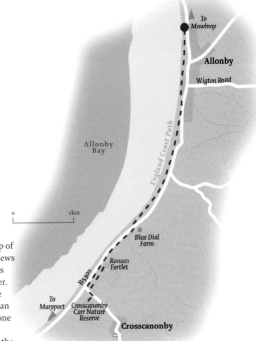

To
Mawbray

Allonby

Wigton Road

Allonby
Bay

◄ Allonby Bay

England Coast Path

0   1km

Blue Dial
Farm

B5300

Roman
Fortlet

To
Maryport   Crosscanonby
Carr Nature
Reserve

Crosscanonby

short way from the top of the hill, from where views of marauding attackers would have been better. However, fortlets were built exactly one Roman mile apart – and this one is no exception.

Looking down from the viewpoint, on the shoreline below are the Anglo-Saxon saltpans, one of the best preserved examples of their type in England. Water gathered in storage tanks would have been boiled to evaporation in pan houses, leaving behind precious salt for preserving foods.

Returning to the roadside path, retrace your steps to Allonby to meander through the streets back to the start. On sunny days, long queues form at Twentymans Ice Cream shop.

Allonby was home between 1958 and 1970 to the artist Percy Kelly (1918-93), whose works have become sought after in recent years. The red bridge was one of his favourite subjects and he lived in a house set back to the right of it as you head northwards. Look for the plaque on the wall facing the road. Kelly drew many scenes in Allonby, all of which are still recognisable. It's notable how little has changed in the intervening years.

33

Crosscanonby and Maryport

Distance 11.5km **Time** 2 hours 30
Terrain footpath, pavement and quiet
lanes **Map** OS Explorer OL4 **Access** buses
from Maryport and Carlisle stop on the
A596 on the upper edge of Crosscanonby,
a 15-minute walk from the start

**This is very much a Roman walk, with
an abundance of history infusing a
countryside and seafront amble around
the village of Crosscanonby and the
fringes of Maryport. Visit one of the
best-preserved defensive fortlet sites
along Hadrian's Wall, wander the course
of an old Roman Road and pop into
Cumbria's only Roman museum.**

Start from the parking area at the small
Crosscanonby Carr Nature Reserve, which
has a mix of wetland habitats. Begin with
a loop of the reserve, keeping an eye open
for barn owl, wildfowl and amphibians.
Back at the car park, turn right to follow
the lane away from the coast as it
gradually climbs up to the village of
Crosscanonby. (Alternatively, to avoid
crossing the golf course, turn left towards

the coast, then left again to follow the
cyclepath, picking up the route described
below at the road to pass the clubhouse.)
There is a bench in the centre of the
village to admire the view back down to
the coast. Continue through the village,
popping in to visit the finely positioned
St John the Evangelist Church. Its interior
was described by the architectural
historian Sir Nikolaus Pevsner as being
'full of good things', and the graveyard
has some marvellous old headstones,
including a Viking 'hogs-back' tomb.

On the edge of the village, turn right at
the bridleway fingerpost, signed for Bank
End, and follow the track down past the
sewage works and then diagonally across
a meadow. At the far corner, go through
the left-hand gate, across the field and
through the next gate, emerging on
Maryport Golf Course. Follow the
bridleway waymarkers across a series of
fairways: the markers can be tricky to
spot in places; just keep heading in the
direction of the arrows when you find
one. Don't linger and be respectful of the

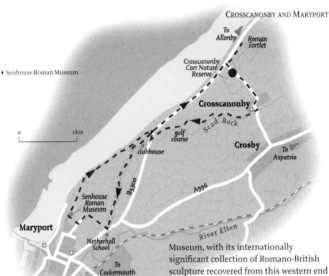

To Allonby

Roman Fortlet

Crosscanonby Carr Nature Reserve

◀ Senhouse Roman Museum

Crosscanonby

Scad Beck

golf course

Crosby

clubhouse

To Aspatria

0   1km

B5300

A596

Senhouse Roman Museum

Maryport

River Ellen

Netherhall School

To Cockermouth

golfers, pausing when they are taking a shot. The bridleway soon follows a stream along the edge of the course, then continues down to the road.

Turn right, cross over and then go left along the road to pass the clubhouse, before turning left along the public byway, signed for Netherhall. This delightful track is lined with thick hedgerows on both sides and gradually climbs to offer fine views in both directions along the coastal route.

At the main road, go right and then immediately right again to climb up the steep footpath steps. The path joins a road for a short distance, and then goes right, signed for the promenade. At the end is the clifftop Senhouse Roman

Museum, with its internationally significant collection of Romano-British sculpture recovered from this western end of Hadrian's Wall World Heritage Site.

Continue along the clifftop path with great views out over the Solway and back to Maryport Harbour. Carry on along the tarmac path that leads down to the sea, at which turn right along the promenade for about 1km, following the England Coast Path waymarker and soon repassing the clubhouse. Once at the road junction, cross over and follow the cycleway for about 2km back to the start.

For a final point of history, once back at the Crosscanonby road, take the track up to the site of Milefortlet 21, one of a series of defensive forts built by the Romans along the Cumbrian coast and a distance of around 1km there and back. This is part of the defensive frontier that includes Hadrian's Wall, and is the only excavated and visible example of its kind.

Maryport

Distance 6km **Time** 2 hours
Terrain pavement and footpaths
Map OS Explorer OL4 **Access** bus to
Maryport from Carlisle; trains to
Maryport from Carlisle, Whitehaven
and Barrow-in-Furness

**Once a centre of shipbuilding and
industry, Maryport is undergoing
something of a regeneration with
bustling streets and a marina packed
with leisure boats. This is a fine town and
waterfront walk with plenty of historical
distractions along the way.**

Starting at the aquarium, follow the
quay round the harbour and marina,
passing along Ismay Wharf and onwards
out to the pier, where fishermen
congregate to cast their lines. Thomas
Ismay, founder of The White Star Line,
was born and lived in Maryport. The inner
docks make up the working port, the
outer the marina, and there's always
plenty of activity to watch from one of
the waterside cafés.

From the pier, walk along the top of the
sea wall back the way you came, with
views across the marina to the town on
one side, out to the Solway and Scotland
on the other, and ahead down the coast to
the wind turbines at Workington. At the
end of the sea wall, go down the steps to
the path and, at a junction of paths,
continue straight on, and then straight on
again where more paths intersect.

On reaching the road, turn left. Head for
the blue bridge across the River Ellen
(Maryport was previously called Ellenfoot)
and, after crossing it, keep to the riverside
path. Ahead lies the harbour and a
striking view of the now deconsecrated
Christ Church, a building painted often,
from various angles, by local artist Percy
Kelly (1918-93).

Maryport

The Alauna Aura, Maryport

At the end of the path, with the Maritime Museum on your right, wander up Senhouse Street to the right, so-named after Humphrey Senhouse II (1706-1770), who founded Maryport in 1756 and named it after his wife, Mary Fleming.

Around 100m up Senhouse Street, turn left up the High Street, then near the top head right down Eaglesfield Street to Fleming Square, named after Mary Fleming's father, George, Bishop of Carlisle. This charming and striking 18th-century cobbled square, surrounded by Georgian and Victorian houses, feels more European in character than British. From the obelisk in the centre of the square a number of themed paths lead off, with descriptions inscribed in the paving stones. Take the Roman Path. Maryport stands on the site of the Roman fort Alauna, constructed as part of the 'Western Sea Defences' on the western boundary of Hadrian's Wall.

Exiting Fleming Square in the top left corner, pause to read the historical texts etched in the glass of the windows of 1 Fleming Place (the first house on the left). The road heads downhill to the left, but keep straight on to join Solway Terrace which runs along the clifftop to the right, passing the excellent Senhouse Roman Museum with its reconstructed watchtower. Beyond the museum, follow the path down to the promenade, where you turn left to return to Maryport, brushing up on your Roman history on the way: each of the benches along the prom is dedicated to a different emperor.

Siddick Ponds and Seaton

Distance 7km Time 1 hour 30
Terrain footpath, cyclepath and
pavement Map OS Explorer 303
Access buses to Dunmail Park from
Carlisle, Maryport and Whitehaven

**It may not have the most auspicious of
beginnings, but this walk soon leaves the
northern edge of industrial Workington
behind to head for the fertile landscape
of Siddick Ponds Local Nature Reserve
and Site of Special Scientific Interest.**

If driving, park at the back of the car
park at Dunmail Park shopping centre, to
the right of the car dealership. From the
car park, head up onto the old mineral
railway embankment, now a cyclepath.
Turn right and then immediately right
down the steps to loop the smaller
brackish pond, a mix of freshwater and
saltwater. Initially, a narrow path through
trees, this soon joins a hard-surface path,
then a rough track behind some
buildings. This goes over a bridge and

along the fence of the playing field to
the steps in the far corner, then back up
to the embankment.

Cross straight over and continue up a
few more steps into a meadow for the
best views over the larger freshwater
pond. Arguably one of the best sites in
Cumbria for birds, this protected site
started life as part of the River Derwent
delta at the tail end of the last ice age.
With the coming of the railway in the
19th century, the embankment cut
through the site thus creating the ponds.

Whatever the season, there is
something to see. Spring is a busy time
with the influx of migratory warblers
such as reed, sedge, grasshopper and
whitethroat filling the air with song.
Winter is also special with the chance to
catch rarities such as the elusive bittern,
an amazing murmuration of starlings or
the squealing call of the shy water rail.
Be sure to bring your binoculars.

Cross the meadow, climb over the stile

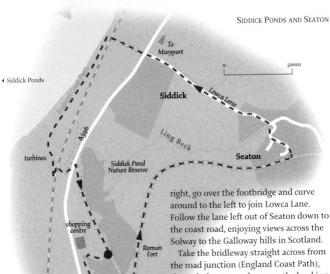

◀ Siddick Ponds

To Maryport

0   500m

Siddick

Lowca Lane

Ling Beck

England Coast Path

A596

turbines

Seaton

Siddick Pond
Nature Reserve

shopping
centre

Roman
Fort

Workington

and turn left to follow the cyclepath for approximately 2km to Seaton. Along the way, there are plenty of reminders of the old railway heritage with fine stone bridges and ornate culverts. Off to the right are the remains of Burrow Walls Roman Fort. On the approach to Seaton village, pass under a bridge arch into a tunnel of trees and, just after the community orchard, turn left into the cul de sac.

For this short section through the housing estate, turn right when you come to the T-junction and follow the road as it curves downhill slightly. At the next T-junction, go right again, then on under the car park height barrier. Head to the

right, go over the footbridge and curve around to the left to join Lowca Lane. Follow the lane left out of Seaton down to the coast road, enjoying views across the Solway to the Galloway hills in Scotland.

Take the bridleway straight across from the road junction (England Coast Path), through the gate and up over the banking. Carefully cross the railway line and go left along the footpath. The mishmash of possible paths for the next 1km can be a bit confusing, but take the footpath along the back of the beach to the right of the broader track. Continue as it climbs the low cliff and runs along the top through the fir trees and heather, with views of wind turbines ahead. Drop down the other side and follow the broad track at the bottom to the left and then go left onto a footpath by the substation. Keep left to join a track by the railway and follow it left until the underpass – mind your head when passing through.

Turn left onto the cyclepath and then right, signed for the town centre. Continue over the bridge crossing the coast road for the final stretch back along Siddick Ponds to the start.

Parton and Harrington

Distance 16km (full loop) or 6km (linear coastal walk between stations)
Time 4 hours **Terrain** pavement, field path, country path **Map** OS Explorer 303
Access bus to Parton from Whitehaven; trains to Parton from Carlisle and Barrow-in-Furness

Diminutive Parton and its larger neighbour, Harrington, bookend an enticing stretch of coast that can only be accessed on foot. The long but easy outward leg of this walk uses the traffic-free National Route 72 but the drama is found on the return. As an alternative, catch the train from Parton to Harrington and just walk the clifftop section back.

From the waterfront parking area next to the railway station at Parton, head north along the beach, then go through the tunnel under the railway. Cross the beck, turn right and take the path on the left uphill. At the top go right to St Bridget's Church, occupying a prominent hilltop position. Near here

stood the Roman fort of Gabrocentum, at the southern end of the string of defences that extended from Hadrian's Wall.

Exiting the churchyard, return along the road to the left, continuing into Lowca. Where Stamford Hill is signposted to the right, take this and then the waymarked path that winds up through the park, emerging at the top onto Solway Road. Go right here and at a junction of paths, keep ahead on the paved road to soon join the designated path on the left.

For the next 3km or so, stay on the cycleway. At the start, pass through an area covered by around eight hectares of glasshouses, part of ornamental plant growers Blomfields. The route further on is lined by trees and runs above the Lowca Beck before dropping down to dip under the A595. The next section runs closer to the busy road but is largely sheltered from it by a high bank.

Stay on the cycleway when it turns left through an underpass below the A595 and, at the next junction, go left again

◄ Parton beach

along a lovely section of overhanging trees. Immediately after passing through the tunnel beneath the road, climb the steps on the left that lead up to the road.

Turn right to follow the road and continue ahead up through the houses and over the brow of the hill, where the Solway comes into view and Scotland beyond. Heading downhill, pass through the traffic-restriction bollards and, just after the public footpath sign off to the right, go up Grayson Green, the unsurfaced lane on the left.

Walk up between the houses and take the track on the right, downhill, immediately after The Retreat. Ignore the footpath sign to the left and carry on downhill to pass a final house on the right, go through a gate and down a surfaced path. Carry on through a kissing gate and down a field path, at the bottom going through another kissing gate and turning right and then first left to follow the path around the school and down to the main street. At the bottom, go left for the harbour, an ideal spot to stop for a break.

To return to Parton, the route follows the England Coast Path. With your back to Harrington Harbour and the public toilets, head out over the grass in front of a house, parallel to Rose Hill. Bear left

almost immediately up the grassy bank to climb the steps, cross over the railway and continue right uphill. The further up you climb the better the views.

Keep ahead, ignoring tracks joining from the left. This is an invigorating stretch, especially when the gorse is in flower. On reaching Lowca, follow the track around to the left and then ahead past the rugby ground. At the main road, turn right downhill and then right again a little further on back down to Parton. Retrace your steps along the beach.

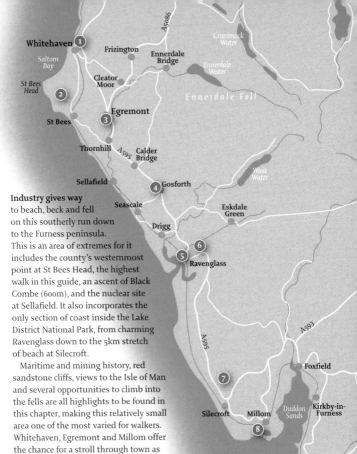

Industry gives way
to beach, beck and fell
on this southerly run down
to the Furness peninsula.
This is an area of extremes for it
includes the county's westernmost
point at St Bees Head, the highest
walk in this guide, an ascent of Black
Combe (600m), and the nuclear site
at Sellafield. It also incorporates the
only section of coast inside the Lake
District National Park, from charming
Ravenglass down to the 5km stretch
of beach at Silecroft.

Maritime and mining history, red
sandstone cliffs, views to the Isle of Man
and several opportunities to climb into
the fells are all highlights to be found in
this chapter, making this relatively small
area one of the most varied for walkers.
Whitehaven, Egremont and Millom offer
the chance for a stroll through town as
part of longer walks, while a wander
through the grounds of Muncaster Castle
takes in one of Cumbria's finest stately
homes, occupied continuously by the
same family for 800 years.

Wildlife features, too, notably in a
limestone quarry nature reserve near
Egremont and birdwatching on the cliffs
around St Bees and in the RSPB's coastal
lagoon at Millom. Key species to look out
for are black guillemot at the former and
great crested grebe at the latter.

Whitehaven to Millom

Whitehaven

Distance **5.5km** Time **1 hour 30**
Terrain **pavement and footpaths**
Map **OS Explorer 303** Access **buses to
Whitehaven from Carlisle, Wigton,
Maryport and Workington; trains to
Whitehaven from Carlisle, Barrow-in-
Furness and Lancaster**

**Whitehaven is a handsome town that
wears its maritime and mining history
with pride. This relatively short walk
along the quaysides, cliffs and Georgian
lanes explores many of its highlights.**

Starting from the railway station, go up
to the main road, turn right, cross at the
pedestrian crossing and go right for the
Millennium Promenade (alternatively cut
across the Tesco car park).

At the *Whiting Shoal* sculpture – a
symbol of how important fishing has

been to the town over the years – head
along the right side of the quay. When
this splits, the North Pier (a dead end)
offers a pleasant detour of Solway views,
or veer left and carry on over the Sea Lock
gates. Note, there is no pedestrian access
across the gates during 'free flow', the
point when the sea level is equal to the
marina basin level and the gates are kept
open. The only option then is to retrace
your steps and walk all the way around
the marina to the other side.

Assuming the gates are closed, cross the
lock, continue along the old quay (mind
your footing on the uneven surface) and
on past the watchtower of around 1730.
At the end of the quay take the steps
under the white tower and along
Wellington Terrace, with its moving
memorial to those that perished in the

Whitehaven

Wellington Pit disaster of 1910. Continue around to the left, up the Coast Path steps and left to arrive at the Candlestick. Coalmining (along with shipbuilding) brought prosperity to Georgian Whitehaven and this is the site of the old Wellington Pit, which closed in 1933. The 'candlestick' is the old boiler house chimney, supposedly modelled on a candlestick belonging to the Lowther family, who owned the pit.

Continue on the Coast Path up the hill and, at its brow, the winding engine house of the old Haig Colliery comes into sight, along with a fine view along the towering cliffs to St Bees North Head. Once level with the old pit, take the path off to the right and peer over the edge to see the ruins of the Saltom Pit. Abandoned in 1848, this was the first undersea coalmine in England.

Retrace your steps to the Candlestick and follow the path past Wellington Lodge. At the small car park, take the downhill path by the compass seat and then go down the steep steps back to the quayside. The Beacon Museum off to the left, with its mix of permanent and changing exhibitions and events, is worth a visit. Alternatively, turn right along West

Strand and just after the Sugar Tongue and the modern 'bandstand', head away from the quay, crossing the main road to the pretty Market Place. Take the road to the left of the Market Hall, then turn left down Queen Street, lined with impressive townhouses, including Gale Mansion, the town's oldest large house, at no 151.

Immediately after the old *Whitehaven News* offices, turn right onto Roper Street and, at the end, either cross to explore tranquil Trinity Gardens or turn left along Scotch Street, keeping an eye open for its interesting doorways.

At the crossroads turn left down Lowther Street, passing the St Nicholas Centre church and tower and Rum Story museum before returning to the marina. Turn right along the promenade and you will soon arrive back at the start.

◀ Whitehaven Harbour

St Bees to Whitehaven

Distance 13km **Time** 3 hours (one way)
Terrain footpaths and pavements
Map OS Explorer 303 **Access** buses to
St Bees from Whitehaven, Egremont and
Millom; trains to St Bees from Carlisle,
Barrow-in-Furness and Lancaster,
returning from Whitehaven by train

This linear hike from the start of
Wainwright's long-distance Coast to
Coast path is arguably Cumbria's most
famous stretch of coastline. Enjoy the
huff and puff of this undulating trail,
which on a clear day offers impressive
views and wildlife spectacles, finishing
at the delightful Whitehaven waterfront.

Exiting left from St Bees Station, cross
the level crossing, carry on over the bridge
and take the footpath on the left, just
before Priory church. Join the road and
follow it down to the beach and the
official start of the Coast to Coast path.
Heading for the big cliffs over to the right,
begin the steep climb up on this well-
trodden trail. Mind your step all along the
route as the path is quite rough in places,
can be overgrown with gorse and thistle
(shorts wearers be warned) and the edge
is never far off. Take particular care if
walking with a dog.

The red sandstone cliffs today rise to
90m and it's hard to imagine that some
250 million years ago, in the Triassic
Period, this would have all been desert.
There are fine views all around, including
to the Isle of Man, 48km off to the west,
the Lakeland fells to the south and east,
and northwards to St Bees Lighthouse.

The first prominent landmark is
Fleswick Bay, which is worth nipping

down to. The pebbly beach with a backdrop of towering cliffs makes for a great pitstop and is far larger than the narrow approach implies. Climb out of the gully on the Coast Path and continue along the top, passing three RSPB observation points, which offer a chance to peer over the edge and take in all the sights (and smells) of the high-rise bird colonies that make this their home. Amongst the many species to look out for are fulmar, kittiwake, peregrine falcon and England's only breeding colony of black guillemot.

Passing St Bees Lighthouse, set slightly inland, carry on along the coast, with the views to Whitehaven and Galloway, in Scotland, opening up before you. At Birkhams Quarry, a source of building stone used from Carlisle to Hong Kong, the path gradually drops down the cliffs. Go left to stay with the Coast Path, initially along the cliff and field edge, and then on the grassy tops. Along this final stretch to Whitehaven, look out for the ruined winding house of Saltom Pit, England's first undersea coalmine, down on the beachside. Up on the clifftop, pass the unmissable winding engine house of the old Haig Colliery.

Enjoying the fine view over Whitehaven,

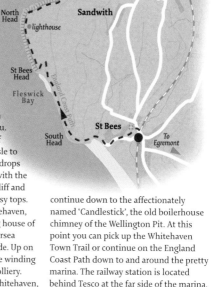

continue down to the affectionately named 'Candlestick', the old boilerhouse chimney of the Wellington Pit. At this point you can pick up the Whitehaven Town Trail or continue on the England Coast Path down to and around the pretty marina. The railway station is located behind Tesco at the far side of the marina.

◄ Coastal path between Whitehaven and St Bees

47

Egremont

Distance **8.5km** Time **2 hours**
Terrain **town streets, riverside and field paths, rough track** Map **OS Explorer 303**
Access **buses to Egremont from Maryport and Whitehaven**

These days Egremont is known primarily for its September Crab Fair (a reference to apples, not crustaceans), but there is much more to this medieval town than at first meets the eye. Local history, wildlife, industrial heritage and an unusual nature reserve are combined in this exceptionally varied walk.

Begin your walk from the castle mound at the southern end of town. Originally Norman, the remains seen today are enough to be able to imagine what it was once like and its history was dramatic enough to inspire Wordsworth to immortalise it in his poem *The Horn of Egremont Castle*. Interpretation boards

around the grounds offer a fuller story.

Heading back to the town, turn left along the Main Street and cross the busy roundabout at the end via the underpass. Note the creative colour-coded tiling representing local geology and haematite deposits, a reference to the town's iron-mining past.

Exiting the underpass, continue ahead along East Road into a residential area. After around 200m, go right down a rough wide track between the houses and then take the narrow path straight ahead downhill to reach the River Ehen. Follow the path to the left along the river for around 1.5km, crossing over the quiet road at Briscoe Mill arched bridge and continuing ahead for a pleasant waterside saunter through the fields. At the end of this stretch, cross the bridge over the river to enter Longlands Lake country park and, where the path splits, go right to walk

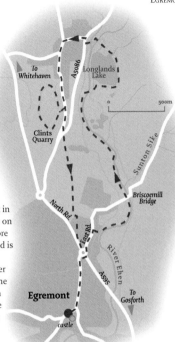

◄ Longlands Lake

part-way round the lake to the car park in an anti-clockwise direction. The lake is on the site of the former Longlands iron ore mine, supports a variety of habitats and is important for its birdlife.

Leave the car park in the far left corner and, after climbing steps up through the woods, go right to emerge on the main road, where the route continues up the road diagonally opposite to your right. Take great care when crossing, as the main road can be busy.

Continue up the road and, after rounding a left-hand corner, head down the road on the left, signposted for Egremont. After about 500m, and immediately after crossing a stone bridge, enter Cumbria Wildlife Trust's Clints Quarry by climbing up some steps on the right, then dropping down into the reserve. Originally a limestone quarry, since 1930 it has been left to recolonise naturally and is now a wildlife haven with flower-rich grassland, woodland, scrub, freshwater ponds and awesome limestone cliffs. A full circuit of the reserve is just under 1km.

Returning to the road, go right and, shortly afterwards, branch off to the left down a route signposted as National Cycle Network 72. Where the path splits, take the left-hand fork, keeping the cemetery ahead on your right and, at the next split in the path, go right. On reaching the main road, cross over and go left, through the bollards and down North Road to return to the town centre.

Gosforth

Distance 6.5km **Time** 1 hour 30
Terrain country lanes, farm track, field
path **Map** OS Explorer OL6 **Access** bus to
Gosforth from Whitehaven

**This straightforward and relatively
short walk punches above its weight
thanks to the breathtaking views of
Ponsonby Fell from the hills above the
pretty village of Gosforth. A fairly steep
but short-lived climb precedes a hearty
ramble across fields and leisurely return
along the valley of the River Bleng.**

From the car park, turn right along the
main street. At the roundabout go right
and then very shortly right again up a
lane between houses. The gentle incline
quite quickly steepens, but it only lasts a
short distance. At Blennerhazel house, go
left up a stretch of grass to a field gate,
where you cross the stile on the right.

Continue straight on along the
hedgeline on your right to cross over
three fields. At the end of the second

field, squeeze through a walkers' gap
in the stone wall and keep straight on,
squeezing through another gap in a wall
and ignoring the path going off to the
right. Views of the coast and fells open
up across this stretch. After crossing the
third field, continue ahead along a path
between two stone walls to reach
Wind Hall Farm.

Wander up the lane to the left for
around 500m. Where it bends to the left
just after an area of plantation forestry, go
right and then immediately right again,
along the track signposted for Whinnerah.
Where the track splits, take the one on the
right into Whinnerah and follow it down
to the farmhouse, soaking up the
outstanding views across the valley, over
Blengdale Forest and up Ponsonby Fell.
On a sunny day it's magic; on a gloomy
one it's moody.

Approaching the farmhouse, keep to the
right of way and follow the waymarkers.
Pass a farm shed on the left, then one on

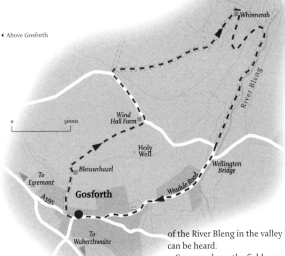

◄ Above Gosforth

Whinnerah

River Bleng

0   500m

Wind
Hall Farm

Holy
Well

Wellington
Bridge

Blennerhazel

Wasdale Road

Gosforth

To
Egremont

A595

To
Waberthwaite

the right and, almost at the farmhouse, take the path to the right down the side of a stone building and go through the gate at the bottom. Head downhill and go through the second, lower of the two gates on the right, as waymarked.

Follow the contoured path downhill, through a gate, then onwards between areas of bracken. In the distance you might hear the hoot of the La'al Ratty Railway at Ravenglass further south. Look out for woodpecker around here, too.

Keep heading downhill with a line of trees immediately on your left. Just beyond the trees, follow the path where it starts to drop more steeply and then switches back on itself. By now the sound

of the River Bleng in the valley bottom can be heard.

Carry on down the field, a mass of buttercups in summer, and then through an area of woodland for the final drop to the valley floor. At the bottom go through the gate and turn right along the lane for the final stretch of around 2.5km back into Gosforth. Much of the route follows the River Bleng; there's a good picnic spot at the water's edge which can be accessed from one of the passing places.

Keep ahead along the lane, ignoring roads off to the right and left. At the main road, carry straight on, following the sign for Gosforth, and enjoy the wander through the village, stopping in at historic St Mary's Church with its eye-catching lychgate. Refreshments await at one of Gosforth's two pubs in the centre of the village.

Ravenglass and Muncaster Castle

Distance 10km **Time** 2 hours 30
Terrain country lanes, rough tracks, field
path, shoreline **Map** OS Explorer OL6
Access bus to Ravenglass from
Whitehaven; trains to Ravenglass from
Carlisle, Barrow-in-Furness and Lancaster

**Idyllic Ravenglass is the only coastal
village in Cumbria that lies within the
boundaries of the national park. Its
charms are evident, from its waterside
setting to its pretty main street and
narrow-gauge steam railway. This
moderate route makes the most of it all
and includes a sojourn through the
grounds of nearby Muncaster Castle, too.**

*The final stretch along the shore is not
passable at high tide; in particular, for two
hours either side of tides above 7.2m. Check
tide tables in advance and time your visit
carefully. An entry charge (reduced for walkers)
is payable to pass through the grounds of
Muncaster Castle.*

Exit the station up the ramp by the
turntable for the narrow-gauge railway.
At the top, go left and, on almost reaching
the main road, continue hard right along

the approach road to the campsite.
Follow the path through the woods,
soon reaching the remains of what was
a bathhouse for the Roman fort of
Ravenglass, dating from around 130AD.

Beyond the bathhouse, where the lane
forks, take the track to the left and follow
it gently uphill. Just before reaching
Newtown farmhouse, take the path to
the left, signposted for the Esk Trail, up
through the woods, passing a pond on
the right. Emerging from the woods,
continue ahead and, on reaching a
junction of roads, keep straight on to
reach the ticket office for Muncaster
Castle, home to the Pennington family
since at least the early 13th century.

Visitors to the castle are charged a fee,
but a reduced price option is available for
walkers passing through. Ask for a
walkers' ticket and, once in the grounds,
keep to the main path, signposted for
the Castle and passing the Wildlife
Garden, Eco Barn and Hawk and Owl
Centre. At the Stable Yard carry on ahead
downhill to the castle itself, to loop round
the southern end of it to the other side,

To
Holmrook

A595

Ravenglass

◀ Looking towards Ravenglass

Muncaster
Castle

Roman Bath
House

Newtown
Farm

Newtown
Knott

River Esk

0   500m

pausing on the way to admire the view of the mountains in the distance.

Carry on along the main path, passing the play area on the right-hand side, and then take the path to the left signposted as a public footpath. Climb up through the woods, ignoring paths going off to the left and right, keeping ahead to a kissing gate in a stone wall at the top. Go through the gate to be greeted by another superb view, looking down over the coast and out to the Isle of Man. Head downhill, in the direction of the signpost, aiming roughly for the stand of trees on the left or the end of the spit of land just offshore. As you near the bottom of the field, look along the fenceline for a stile.

Cross the stile and follow the path down through the woods, emerging at the outbuildings of Newtown Farm. Go left, passing the farm buildings, and on through a farm gate at the top of the rise. Cross the field and, at a junction of tracks, take the right-hand one to climb up and around Newtown Knott.

On rounding the Knott, drop down to the right through a gate and head straight downhill across the field. Towards the other side, veer right slightly where the ground falls away and look for a gate hidden behind an area of gorse. Once through the gate, go left and then right on a permitted path to reach the shoreline, at which go right again.

It's now a case of following the shore all the way back to Ravenglass, revelling in the coastal views of the sandbars and Ravenglass in the distance. In summer, the grasses on either side of the path grow taller than head height and for short stretches you're hidden from the surrounding landscape. Look out for jellyfish along the shoreline.

On reaching Ravenglass, you can either continue along the shore or turn right up the Main Street. Towards the end of the street, cut up the alley alongside the Pennington Hotel, cross over the road at the top and continue ahead to cross the railway and drop back down into the station car park.

53

Muncaster Fell and Eskdale Green

Distance **15km** Time **3 hours 30**
Terrain **rough tracks, fell path, lanes**
Map **OS Explorer OL6** Access **bus to
Muncaster from Whitehaven; trains to
Ravenglass from Carlisle, Barrow-in-
Furness and Lancaster**

**This moderately difficult walk crosses
the long steep-sided ridge of Muncaster
Fell, only 231m at its highest but with
fine views to the bigger Lakeland Fells.
The distant hoot of the steam train on
the narrow-gauge Ravenglass and
Eskdale Railway punctuates the air
periodically, conjuring up images of days
past in this timeless setting.**

The walk begins from the car park at
Muncaster Castle's main gate (a donation
is requested for parking here). Take the
path from the top right-hand corner of the
car park, signposted Esk Trail, and follow
it through the field and up to the road,
before then heading up Fell Lane on the
left. At Muncaster Tarn (private), take the
path to the right and keep ahead. Ignore
the Esk Trail path that joins from the right
and head uphill with views of the tarn,
covered in waterlilies, below to the left.
Around here in summer, look out for
ringlet butterflies, a lovely velvety
chocolate brown colour with distinctive
ring markings on their wings.

Emerging from the surrounding trees
onto the fell at the top of the path, the
landscape opens up with glorious hill
views. With the cairn on top of Hooker
Crag in clear view ahead, carry on,
following the fenceline on the left until
it swings away to the left, at which point
take the path that veers to the right.
At the next split in the path, head uphill
to the left to climb up to the cairn, a great
spot to stop for sandwiches and enjoy the
expansive 360-degree views, out to sea
over Ravenglass in one direction and into
the Lake District mountains in the other.

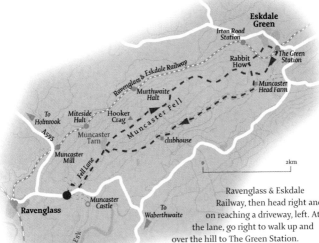

Dropping back down to the path, continue in the direction of Eskdale Green. A succession of paths takes off in different directions as you cross the fell. Generally keep to the middle and right of the fell, taking paths that in summer are almost obscured by bracken. In due course, the path cuts through a break in a drystone wall and heads downhill. Follow the line of the wall on the left for around 250m, then keep to the path as it veers away from the wall before looping around to the right. Ahead in the distance are the houses of Eskdale Green.

The path climbs again as it meanders around Rabbit How before a straight stretch descends to a gate in a stone wall, where you go left. Shortly after, take the path to the right to cross the line of the

Ravenglass & Eskdale Railway, then head right and, on reaching a driveway, left. At the lane, go right to walk up and over the hill to The Green Station.

Crossing the line again, take the path off to the right. Go through a farm gate and follow the line of the wall on the right. Where it takes a right turn, continue diagonally right across the field to the gate on the far side, at which follow the track left down to Muncaster Head Farm. Continue with the farm buildings on your left and, at the gateway, go right to pick up the Esk Trail.

Follow the trail for around 45 minutes, passing through an area of commercial forestry and on past the Eskdale Golf Course and clubhouse. Look out for an Esk Trail signpost, where you take the track on the right uphill for a steep lengthy climb of around 750m – testing on the legs at this final stage. At the top, the path emerges at Muncaster Tarn, where you go left to rejoin the outward leg and retrace your steps to the start.

◀ View from Muncaster Fell

Black Combe

Distance 8.5km **Time** 3 hours
Terrain footpaths and open hill
Map OS Explorer OL6 **Access** trains to
Silecroft from Carlisle, Barrow-in-Furness
and Lancaster

Tucked away in the far southwest of
the Lake District National Park, Black
Combe rises abruptly from the lush
coastal plains along the Irish Sea. This
exhilarating route on a clear path offers
a good workout and great views. It is
not advisable to attempt this in poor
visibility. Come prepared for all weather,
too: lighter clothing that might suffice
on the lower reaches can quickly feel
inadequate; a hat, waterproofs and
multiple layers are recommended.

Begin at the lay-by on the A5093 near
the A595 junction. Turning right out of
the lay-by, take the footpath just a short
distance along on the left, signed for

Black Combe. Cross the field and go left
up to the main road. Once over the road,
follow the footpath diagonally across to
the corner where the stone wall and
hedge meet, then continue over the next
field, aiming to the right of the house.
Go left along the narrow lane, taking the
path running behind the house and up
through the large wooden gate. You're
now in the Lake District National Park.

The footpath immediately climbs up
into the hills, initially passing between
Seaness on the left and Moor Gill on the
right. Of Black Combe, Wainwright
famously asked 'Which other fell can be
ascended in carpet slippers?' While the
path is certainly clear, sturdier footwear
is definitely recommended.

Having started near sea level, height
is soon gained and fine views open up.
Keep an eye and ear open for ravens
and the clack of stonechat sitting atop

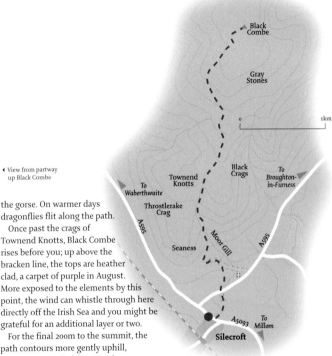

◀ View from partway up Black Combe

the gorse. On warmer days dragonflies flit along the path.

Once past the crags of Townend Knotts, Black Combe rises before you; up above the bracken line, the tops are heather clad, a carpet of purple in August. More exposed to the elements by this point, the wind can whistle through here directly off the Irish Sea and you might be grateful for an additional layer or two.

For the final 200m to the summit, the path contours more gently uphill, invoking a wonderful sense of remoteness, with views stretching north along the coast. Just before the top, the path takes a sharp switch to the left before curving right for the final climb. The summit is quite broad, marked with a triangulation pillar surrounded by a wall which offers welcome shelter on blowy days. Take in the fine 360-degree views over vast swathes of the Lakeland Fells and coast and, if it's a particularly clear day, the Isle of Man and the Mountains of Mourne in Northern Island.

When ready, simply retrace your steps to the start, savouring the coastal views, which take in Millom and Hodbarrow Nature Reserve and Walney Island.

Millom and Hodbarrow

Distance 11km **Time** 2 hours 30
Terrain town streets, country lanes,
unsurfaced tracks, field paths
Map OS Explorer OL6 **Access** trains to
Millom from Carlisle, Barrow-in-Furness
and Lancaster

**Nestling between fell and coast, Millom
may come as a surprise. Southwest
Cumbria's hidden gem is a friendly town
surrounded by exceptional countryside.
This eye-opening circular route
incorporates a delightful museum,
estuary walking and a turn around the
RSPB's artificial freshwater lagoon.**

The Heritage & Arts Centre at Millom
Station provides the perfect introduction
to this walk. If arriving by car, from the
public car park turn right, then right again
over the railway line and right again to
reach the station building. The centre
consists of a series of rooms offering
easily digested bite-sized chunks of
information about the town and
surrounding area, presented in an

engaging way. Local and rural heritage,
the Bronze Age, RAF Millom, a traditional
cottage and shop, Millom's iron-mining
history and the town's most famous son,
poet Norman Nicholson, are all covered.

From the station, cross the bridge and
turn left down Lancashire Road. At the
end of the road, keep ahead and take
the England Coast Path to the right,
signposted for Hodbarrow.

From here on, for almost the entire
route, just keep to the Coast Path, which
runs down the side of the estuary, rounds
the point, skirts the beach and cuts
through to RSPB Hodbarrow, regularly
signposted or waymarked the whole way.

Almost immediately on joining the
path, views of the estuary and Duddon
Sands are laid out before you. At low tide,
the expanse of sand is simply vast. Look
back towards the town and the peaks of
Black and White Combe lead the eye on to
the Cumbrian mountains in the distance.

Roughly 1km after joining the path, cut
into Millom Ironworks Local Nature

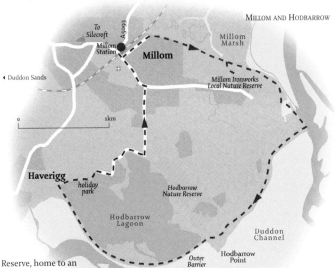

To
Silecroft
A5093
Millom
Station
Millom
Millom
Marsh
◄ Duddon Sands
Millom Ironworks
Local Nature Reserve
0   1km
Haverigg
holiday
park
Hodbarrow
Nature Reserve
Hodbarrow
Lagoon
Duddon
Channel
Hodbarrow
Point
Outer
Barrier

Reserve, home to an array of butterflies and notable for its bee orchids, yellow-wort and natterjack toads. Climb the path to the top for a good vantage point from which to survey the scene. After an anticlockwise stroll around the top, drop back down to the main waterside path.

On reaching the dunes after another 2km, you have a choice of either turning right through the signposted kissing gate to walk along the inside fenceline of a field, or dropping down to walk along the sand and shingle beach. If opting for the latter, you'll need to nip back into the field further along in order to access Hodbarrow Nature Reserve.

At the end of the field, go through a kissing gate and follow the path through the trees. Without warning, Hodbarrow Lagoon comes into view, an impressive sight with its defensive sea wall arcing across to Haverigg. The lagoon occupies the site of an old mine, which was constructed after the discovery of iron ore in 1855. Bringing jobs and prosperity, it boosted the local population to 10,000 souls before closing in 1968. Today, the lagoon is the only nesting place in the Duddon Estuary of the rare little tern.

At the end of the sea wall, go right along the edge of the holiday village and then take the path to the left, signposted as a public byway, up behind the houses. At the top, go left again and stay on this lane for around 1km. On reaching the main road, turn left again back into town. At the first junction, cross over to wander up the main street before going left up St George's Terrace to the market square, at which continue right to return to either the station or car park.

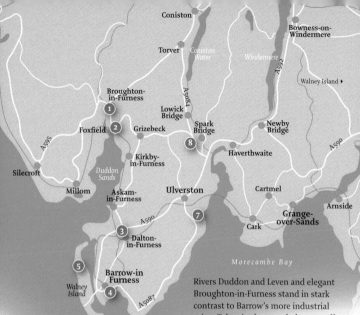

While Cumbria's northern coast faces more towards Carlisle, the southern reaches look to Lancaster. Historically, all of this area formed the most northerly part of Lancashire, specifically the northwest section of the Lonsdale Hundred. Today, the Furness Peninsula incorporates Cumbria's most southerly point and in parts has an unexpected feeling of remoteness, especially in the northern and southern extremities of Walney Island. Pretty stone villages, priory ruins, the superb estuaries of the

Rivers Duddon and Leven and elegant Broughton-in-Furness stand in stark contrast to Barrow's more industrial mien. Taken in the round, the area offers a stimulating mix of grand views, windswept headlands, intriguing history, rare habitats and varied wildlife.

If visiting Barrow, a tour of the superb Dock Museum, housed partly in a conversion of an old dry dock and which tells the town's story, is recommended. Its collection of scale models of ships built here is particularly impressive.

It's worth noting the distinction between Low Furness and High Furness as you're likely to come across both. Low Furness refers to the peninsula itself, delineating the western side of Morecambe Bay, while High Furness lies north of the peninsula, includes the Furness Fells and falls mostly within the Lake District National Park.

The Furness Peninsula

Broughton-in-Furness

Distance 5km **Time** 1 hour 30
Terrain pavement, country lanes and
footpaths **Map** OS Explorer OL6
Access very infrequent bus to Broughton-
in-Furness from Coniston

**Encircled by hills and centred on an
elegant Georgian market square with
commemorative obelisk, the little town
of Broughton-in-Furness has a feel quite
unlike any other in this neck of the
woods. Explore its graceful streets full of
quirky features and signs of yesteryear,
before taking this wander along the
pretty back lanes and countryside.**

First up, explore the town and its main
square with the three-storey merchant
houses, old stocks and fishmarket slabs.
When ready to move on, leave the square
by heading downhill on Market Street, to
the right of the Manor Arms pub. Pass
Foxfield Road and start to climb uphill. At
the primary school and Kepplewray

Centre, turn right to follow the footpath
along a lovely lane between stone walls in
the direction of Eccle Riggs, with fine
views out over Black Combe and the fells.

Continue on through a tiny hamlet of
pretty cottages, pass Gardeners Cottage
and take the path to the left of the last
stone cottage. Follow the footpath
fingerpost and then the waymarkers
across the golf course. Once over the
fairways and at the bottom of the hill by
the treeline, take the path heading hard
left over a tiny stream (no waymarker),
rather than continuing on ahead past the
leisure club. Aim for and go through the
wooden gate in the stone wall.

Follow the path straight ahead uphill,
through the next gate, pausing to enjoy
the views behind of Duddon Estuary.
Once at the lane, turn left. (If linking
into the Duddon Mosses walk, go right at
this point down past Foxfield Bank to the
A595 main road.) At the road junction,

◀ Back Lane

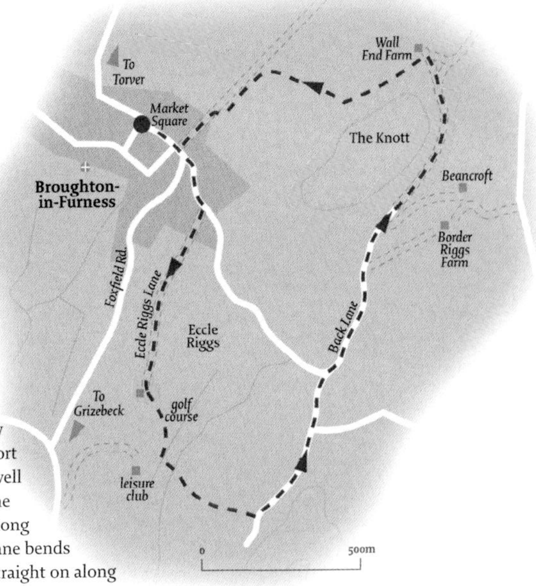

continue carefully downhill for a short stretch, keeping well into the side as the traffic can whip along here. Where the lane bends sharp left, carry straight on along what is known as Back Lane and is signed for Beancroft. This delightful stretch meanders initially through oak and later more mixed broadleaf woodland. Continue on the lane, passing the turning for Beancroft and, just before entering Wall End Farm, take the footpath on the left.

The path leads along the stone wall; look for a 'squeeze stile' in the wall at the end of the horse paddocks, keeping an eye open as it's down a slight embankment and can be tricky to spot amidst the vegetation. Follow the field edge along the stone wall, up over the brow of the slight hill and down the other side.

Pass through the metal gate or squeeze stile (depending on which is most accessible) and curve left to follow the field edge. At the end of the field, climb over the stone steps to join the bridleway, which was once the railway line between Foxfield and Coniston. Opened in 1859, it was initially for passenger traffic but shortly after for the movement of mined minerals.

Turn left to follow the bridleway back to Market Street, then right to head back up to the square, where there are numerous shops to explore, plus pubs and cafés for some post-walk refreshment.

63

Foxfield and Duddon Mosses

Distance 5km (from Foxfield Station) or 10km (from Broughton-in-Furness) **Time** 1 hour 30 **Terrain** pavement, country lane, footpaths **Map** OS Explorer OL6 **Access** infrequent bus to Foxfield from Coniston; trains to Foxfield from Barrow-in-Furness and Carlisle

Duddon Mosses National Nature Reserve lies just to the south of the pretty town of Broughton-in-Furness and more or less next to Foxfield Station. For a longer walk, you can make your way from Broughton by following the start of the previous route, enjoying views down over the Duddon Estuary along the way.

From Foxfield Station, cross over the A595 and turn right, sticking to the pavement for just under 500m. Along the way you will pass a lane on the left, signposted for the Cumbria Coastal Way.

(If you started from Broughton, this is where you will join the route.)

Just before the pavement ends, cross back over the main road to take a dead-end lane on the right, signposted for the public footpath to Angerton Moss. Head down the lane, cross the bridge and keep more or less straight ahead, ignoring the track to the left and the signed footpath to Angerton Moss off to the right.

After passing two cottages, continue ahead to enter Duddon Mosses Reserve, part of an extensive peatland area with lowland raised peatbogs that are amongst the most important in the UK and Europe. The peat here is thought to be around 7000 years old and up to 6m deep. As well as the possibility of spotting adders and lizards, cotton-grass, bog asphodel, bog rosemary, carnivorous sundews and rare sphagnum mosses can be found here.

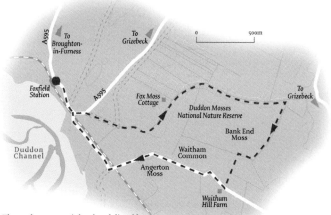

The path runs straight ahead, lined by birch trees, gradually turning east around Bank End Moss (moss is another name for a raised bog). Along the way, pass two other paths – the first to the right, the second to the left – heading out over the bog on boardwalks. For a view of the open landscape, take a wander down either path before returning to the main route. Look out for adders and lizards basking in the sun on the boardwalk.

Keep following the path onwards until you reach a kissing gate into a field, at which stick to the main path as it turns sharp right, heading southwest down the far side of Bank End Moss. At a junction of paths, where Waitham Hill Farm comes into view ahead, take the path to the right, cross over the bridge and keep straight ahead to go through a gate in the middle of the field. Go through another two gates and pass to the left of the farm buildings to reach a lane.

Continue right at the lane and after about 500m there's another chance to pop back into the reserve on the right for a quick explore up the path if you wish. This stretch has sizeable clumps of bog asphodel amongst the heather, with bright yellow flowers in summer and rich rust-red leaves in autumn.

As you carry on down the lane, keep ahead and ignore the path off to the right. Cross over the railway line and emerge on the eastern side of the vast Duddon Estuary, with superb views over Duddon Sands to Millom to the southwest. Turn right along the path and, on reaching the houses, follow the path up to the right to cross back over the railway line. Go left and then either take the signposted path uphill on the right to return to Broughton-in-Furness or continue along the pavement to Foxfield Station.

Dalton-in-Furness and Furness Abbey

Distance 8km **Time** 2 hours
Terrain town streets, footpaths, fields;
can be muddy **Map** OS Explorer OL6
Access buses to Dalton-in-Furness from
Windermere and Kendal; trains to Dalton
from Barrow-in-Furness and Lancaster

Dalton-in-Furness retains an air of civic
significance, thanks to its castle, church
and notable buildings in the old market
square. Founded in 1123, nearby Furness
Abbey was once a great seat of wealth
and power. Both are visited on this varied
walk which also climbs to the hilltop
village of Newton with its extensive
views of the surrounding countryside.

Dalton Castle was built originally as
a peel tower, a small fortified keep in
which the monks from the abbey could
seek refuge from marauding Scots.
Approaching the tower up Market Street,
cut up its left-hand side to head down

Church Street and pass the striking red
sandstone St Mary's Church, dating from
1885. In the churchyard is the grave of
Dalton's most famous son, 18th-century
portrait painter George Romney.

Beyond the church, follow the lane
down to Goose Green. At the bottom of
the hill, keep ahead and bear right along
a lane just before reaching the main road,
then go left over a bridge across the Poaka
Beck to follow a footpath. Keep to the
path for around 1.25km until you come
to a road, at which cross over to another
path along the pretty Vale of Nightshade.
Where the path emerges at a lane, carry
on ahead to pass through a stone arch at
the imposing ruins of Furness Abbey,
the scale of which bears testimony to
the abbey's historic status.

To visit the abbey grounds, go to the
ticket office in the car park. To continue
walking, stick to the lane along the right-

hand side of the ruins. Rounding the far end of the site, where the lane starts to climb uphill, take the path through the woods to the right. Cross the railway line, pass through a gate and bear right to follow the line of the railway and Mill Beck. Continue to the far end of the field and the three-arched Bow Bridge. Dating from the 15th century, it lay on one of the most important trading routes in medieval England.

Exit the field onto the road and go left uphill to the next junction, at which take the path on the right up over the hill. At the top, continue on through the gate across the next field, signposted for Dalton.

Emerging onto the road at Newton, bear diagonally right in front of the pub and follow the road around to the left to pass along the street. Towards the end of the village, just after the Farmer's Arms pub, take the lane uphill to the left, which passes a couple of houses before narrowing to a hedge-lined path. After about 750m, carry straight on where the path broadens to a track, and then continue ahead, over a stile, where the track bends to the right.

Keep on directly ahead, over the next stile and straight on to the road at the far side of the field. Cross over and continue

directly ahead, following a path between and behind houses until you reach a junction of paths, at which go left. Where the path emerges at a playpark, go left down the street and then left again along Coronation Drive. On reaching the main road, either go right down the road or cross over and work your way downhill through the cemetery.

At the bottom of the hill, cross the road and take the path up the left-hand side of the public garden for the return climb to the castle.

Barrow to Roa Island

Distance 5km (one way to Roa)
Time 1 hour 30 (one way)
Terrain paved path **Map** OS Explorer OL6
Access bus to Barrow-in-Furness from
Kendal; trains to Barrow-in-Furness
Station, 1km from the start; it is possible
to return to Barrow, Coniston or
Ulverston by bus from Roa Island

Barrow-in-Furness, Cumbria's second
largest settlement, lies at the southern
tip of the county's southernmost
peninsula, surrounded by water on three
sides and backed by mountains.

A combination of its enviable location
and thriving iron and steel industries
in the 19th century led to the town
becoming one of the country's leading
shipyards. Since the Second World War,
Barrow has produced oil tankers, ocean
liners, submarines and several Royal Navy
flagships, and today shipbuilding remains
the single biggest local employer.

This easy walk skirts several docks
before edging along the shore with

gasworks on one side and the impressive
Duddon Estuary on the other, and finally
crossing the causeway to Roa Island. On a
sunny day it makes for a pleasant jaunt,
offering some grand views across the
mudflats to Walney Island. Walk one way,
have a café lunch, then retrace your steps
or catch the bus.

If driving, begin at Morrison's car park
in Barrow (charge). Exit via the quayside
gate at the rear of the car park, turn left
and just keep following the waterside
path. At the outset, walk along Buccleuch
Dock, one of the four docks which make
up the port of Barrow. The complex of
warehouses and Victorian dock buildings
opposite is now part of BAE Systems who,
following a convoluted process of
mergers and acquisitions, are the owners
of what was once Vickers, historically one
of the most renowned names in British
engineering and military manufacturing.

At the end of Buccleuch Dock keep
ahead between Cavendish Dock on the
left and Ramsden Dock on the right.

Cavendish is now a reservoir and a popular local fishing spot. On reaching the gates at the end, go left along the end of the reservoir, with expansive views on the right out over Roosecote Sands to Piel and Walney Islands, all part of the Duddon Estuary SSSI, an internationally important Ramsar wetlands site. Look out for oystercatcher, dunlin, knot and curlew. In winter, large flocks of wading birds gather here.

Crossing the reservoir, keep ahead, ignoring the path branching off to the left. At the end, go right, again ignoring paths branching off on the left, to pass the gasworks, where gas from the Morecambe Bay and Irish Sea gasfields comes ashore. Soon, views to Roa Island open up. On reaching the road at Rampside, turn right to cross the causeway.

Just under halfway across the causeway, a separate pedestrian causeway branches off to the left, to Cumbria Wildlife Trust's Foulney Island Nature Reserve, an island formed entirely of pebbles from the Lake District brought to the coast by glaciers during the last ice age. Arctic and little tern breed here during the summer. A walk to the end of the island and back from the car park is around 4.5km. Note that around high tide the island may be cut off for several hours.

Continue to Roa Island, with its good views over to diminutive 20-hectare Piel Island, site of a ruined 14th-century castle and of a popular pub, whose landlord is traditionally known as the King of Piel. A privately-run ferry operates to Piel between Easter and October. To return, simply retrace your steps or catch a bus.

◀ Piel Channel and Piel Island

North Walney

Distance 12km **Time** 2 hours 30
Terrain surfaced path, beach or shoreline,
field path **Map** OS Explorer OL6
Access bus to Walney Island from
Barrow-in-Furness

A shoreline of shingle on the west and
mudflats on the east encircles the
northern half of Walney Island, while the
interior is a curious mix of residential
streets, the BAE-owned airfield and the
nationally important North Walney
National Nature Reserve. This is a wild,
windy and captivating place of ever-
changing moods as the weather sweeps
in off the Irish Sea – perfect for blowing
away the cobwebs.

Starting from the parking area at
Sandy Gap on the west shore, the route
forms part of the England Coast Path and
is well waymarked the whole way round,
with a 5km run up to the northernmost
point, followed by 6km down the eastern
shore. The final 1km cutting back over

to the west completes the circuit neatly.

Heading up the western shore, the Irish
Sea rolls into the shingle beach, white
horses ruffling the surface as far as you
can see, with the bulk of Black Combe
further north in the background. Along
the shore look out for large flocks of
oystercatchers. After around 2km, pause
at Earnse Bay's sand and shingle beach,
popular with windsurfers and kitesurfers.
There are also public toilets here.

Continue up the shoreline and soon
the tower at the airfield comes into view
ahead to the right. Follow the path as it
bears right, where signposted, heading
inland slightly away from the shore.
Blackberries and wild rocket can be found
along here in autumn. A network of paths
runs from here to the north of the island;
if in doubt, just keep heading northwards
and bearing right until you are following
the path up the side of the airfield.

Beyond the airfield, enter the North
Walney National Nature Reserve, one of

the country's best coastal reserves with rare habitats such as sand dunes, dune heath, hay meadows and saltmarsh. It's also one of only around 40 sites in England where you can find rare natterjack toads. Come at dusk in spring and you might hear the distinctive rasping mating call of the males. Rare plants found here include the leafless coralroot orchid, dune helleborine and the pale-pink-flowered Walney geranium, all best spotted between June and September. A wide range of bird species might also be seen, including knot, ringed plover, dunlin and curlew.

The path leads through the reserve, skirting the lagoons and on up to the northernmost part of the island, at which it curves around to the right to cross over to the eastern shore. Keep following the waymarkers as they lead you across a couple of fields and back down the airfield's eastern perimeter fence. In autumn, gin enthusiasts might want to forage for sloeberries here.

After passing through a section of old woodland, the path splits, with a summer routing to the left, and a winter and alternative high tide route to the right. The latter should be used from September to March inclusive to avoid disturbing rare

nesting birds along the shoreline.

To follow the summer route, simply drop down to the shore, turn right and continue until the shore reaches the road at North Scale. However, do check tide times as parts of this section are impassable at high tide.

For the winter route, continue along the path to the right, cross over fields and then turn left down the lane through North Scale to reach the shore, where the summer route emerges. From here, carry on down the waterside to Jubilee Bridge and turn right up Central Drive for the final leg back to the start.

◀ Black Combe from Walney Island

South Walney

Distance **10.5km** Time **2 hours 30**
Terrain **quiet lanes and footpaths**
Map **OS Explorer OL6** Access **bus to
Walney Island from Barrow-in-Furness**

**Walney Island has a distinct feel of wild
isolation, a world away from its only
approach through the industrial and
urban areas of Barrow. From its extremity
jutting into the Irish Sea, a varied walk of
habitats, views and birdlife awaits.**

For drivers, there is parking off Thorny
Nook Lane. From the car park, turn right
onto the narrow lane to the village of
Biggar, named from the Norse *bygg* and
geiri, meaning 'a piece of land triangular in
shape where barley grows'. At the village
beacon, turn right onto Mawflat Lane,
waymarked for Snab Point.

Depending on the time of year, the
route takes a different direction after
about 200m. If walking between 1 April
and 31 August, turn left along the
footpath down to the foreshore, following
it for 1.5km to loop around and rejoin the
lane a little further on, but do check the
tide times. The seasonality is because the
shore is a protected area for winter
migrating birds. If walking in autumn and
winter, continue along the lane – this is
generally quiet, but be aware of traffic.

The foreshore path rejoins the lane to
continue down the eastern side of the
island, with expansive views beneath
huge skies in all directions. The saltmarsh
is a mass of tidal channels, full of sea
aster and sea lavender, a perfect habitat
for wading birds like curlew and
redshank. Across the Piel Channel, you
can see Roa Island and Piel Island.

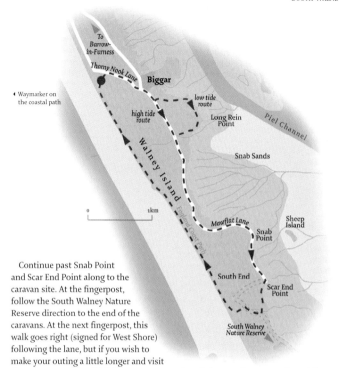

To
Barrow-
in-Furness

Thorny Nook Lane

Biggar

low tide
route

high tide
route

Long Rein
Point

Piel Channel

Walney Island

Snab Sands

Piel Coast Path

0   1km

Mowflat Lane

Snab
Point

Sheep
Island

◄ Waymarker on
the coastal path

South End

Scar End
Point

South Walney
Nature Reserve

Continue past Snab Point and Scar End Point along to the caravan site. At the fingerpost, follow the South Walney Nature Reserve direction to the end of the caravans. At the next fingerpost, this walk goes right (signed for West Shore) following the lane, but if you wish to make your outing a little longer and visit the nature reserve and lighthouse, continue ahead.

Leave the lane, turning left at the next fingerpost (signed for Thorny Nook Lane) to follow the path along the back of the beach. The route to the start simply follows the green National Trail waymarker discs for 4km along the low cliffs, but don't venture too close to their crumbling edge. In spring and summer, the shingle beach is home to nesting

ringed plover and oystercatcher, while in autumn you'll see the fungi, shaggy inkcap, everywhere. Out to sea, the wind turbines are unmissable and make up one of the world's largest offshore windfarms, while ahead the dominant hill rising from the coastal plains is Black Combe.

Along this stretch enjoy the isolation, the crashing waves and bracing winds from the Irish Sea, before arriving back at the start.

Ulverston Sands and Birkrigg Common

Distance 14.5km Time 3 hours 30
Terrain country lanes, field paths, farm
track, shoreline Maps OS Explorer OL6
and OL7 Access buses to Ulverston Sands
from Barrow-in-Furness and Ulverston

**Explore the rolling hills and shoreline of
the central Furness Peninsula just south
of Ulverston. This walk is something of a
southern Cumbrian classic, combining
views, ancient history, livestock farms
and geology, not to mention a visit to a
Buddhist temple.**

From the beachside car park on the
A5087 coast road below Bardsea, climb
gently up into the pretty village via the
access road to the right of the public
toilets. At the top, turn right into Bardsea
and then take the first left, shortly after
bearing left where the lane divides. Pass
the houses and keep on uphill on a path
up the southern edge of Hag Wood.

At the top of the wood, go through a
gate and continue directly ahead. On the

left just down the hill lies the Bronze Age
Druids' Circle, one of only 30 concentric
stone circles in the UK and the only one
in Cumbria.

A little further on, turn right up the
surfaced roadway and pass between the
houses. Ignore the bridleway to Scales off
to the left and continue uphill for around
150m before bearing right towards the top
of the common on a signposted path (this
can be difficult to spot in summer when
the bracken is high).

Follow the path uphill, bearing left
where it splits, and at the brow head right
to the trig point, a good picnic spot with
360-degree views to the fells of the Lake
District to the north and the expanse of
Morecambe Bay to the east and south.
Birkrigg's extensive limestone pavement
bears testimony to the glacial retreat of
around 18,000 years ago.

Continue northwards, with the
distinctive monument to Sir John Barrow
on Hoad Hill above Ulverston in your line

◀ Ulverston Sands

Ulverston

Oakwood Drive

Brick Kiln Road

Croftlands

A5087

Ulverston Channel

The Grange

Middle Mount Barrow Farm

Priory Road

Far Mount Barrow Farm

golf course

meditation centre

Bardsea Park

Bardsea

Birkrigg Common

Hag Wood

stone circle

A5087

Ulverston Sands

To Barrow-in-Furness

0   1km

of sight straight ahead. A network of paths drops down the common; take any one, keeping generally in the direction of the monument and making for an enclosed path between hedgerows running across the bottom of the valley.

On reaching a surfaced road, look for a signposted path with a fingerpost for Far Mount Barrow. Take the enclosed path across the fields and at a lane go right, then left up the driveway to Middle Mount Barrow farm. Pass to the right of the farm buildings and follow the lane round to The Grange, now taking the path up its right-hand side and across a field to a housing estate.

A quick walk connects to the next section of the route: go right along Parkhead Road, right along Birchwood Drive and right down Oakwood Drive. Turn right into Larch Grove and go immediately left into Larch Court, heading diagonally to the near right-hand corner and exiting the Court via a gate in the hedge into the cemetery. Go left downhill through the cemetery and at the road go right for around 500m before taking a path across fields to the left.

Cross a stile and follow the fenceline on the right around the field.

On reaching a lane (Brick Kiln Road), turn right and follow it all the way to the end and a superb viewpoint looking out over Cartmel Sands with a conveniently-placed bench to pause for a moment. From here it's a straightforward 2km jaunt southwards along the shoreline back to the start, with uplifting views the whole way. Along the way, you can pop into the Kadampa Buddhist Centre, with its striking temple and sunny café, using the permissive path up through the woods.

Lowick Common

Distance 9.5km Time 2 hours 30
Terrain footpath, farm track, quiet lanes
Maps OS Explorer OL6 and OL7
Access buses to Spark Bridge from
Coniston and Barrow-in-Furness

Cumbria Wildlife Trust's Lowick
Common forms the centrepiece of this
pretty High Furness walk. A lowland of
heath, grassland and fen areas, it's dotted
with ponds that are home to the rare
medicinal leech, the largest of the
leeches found in the UK and the only
one known to feed on human blood.

The River Crake flows through the
centre of Spark Bridge, 6.4km from
Coniston Water and just inside the
southern boundary of the Lake District
National Park. From the bridge, walk up
the lane to the Farmers Arms by the
A5092. At the road, go left past the

houses, then take the lane that runs
uphill on the right.

On reaching South Woodend, ignore the
footpath to the left and instead veer right
on a walled track along the right-hand
side of a house. Keep ahead down to Beck
Bottom. At the lane, go left downhill
between the cottages and stick to it where
it bends back on itself uphill. At the brow,
go sharp left, doubling back on yourself,
and keep to the lane for around 500m.

Where a track drops down to the left,
take a signposted path to the right to start
the climb up Lowick Beacon, shortly after
taking the left fork to round the northern
side of the Beacon. Keep climbing for the
short but steep ascent to the top. The
Beacon is only 211m high but offers fine
views to the Coniston Fells.

From the top of the Beacon, head back
down on the northwards path, dropping

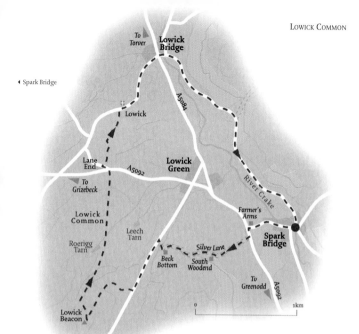

◀ Spark Bridge

down into a hollow and following the waymarker to climb up the other side. Carry on along the path as it runs parallel to a stone wall on the left and then veers off to the right to cross the common, heading almost due north. In summer, keep an eye open for yellowhammers, small pearl-bordered fritillary butterflies and adders.

On reaching the A5092, continue on the path across the road, down to the lane and the hamlet of Lane End. Take the next path on the right between two houses, where signposted, and at the bottom of the hill go through the left-hand gate into

a field. Follow the line of the wall on the right and go through the next gate, then continue across the next field, making for St Luke's Church, visible ahead.

At the lane, turn right past the church. St Luke's dates from 1885 and its extensive churchyard offers a peaceful spot to pause and take in the Old Man of Coniston and the rolling fells of the Crake Valley. A little further along the lane stands the Red Lion pub, once frequented by Arthur Ransome, who lived in the area while writing *Swallows and Amazons*.

Emerging at the main road, cross straight over and follow the lane for 2km back to Spark Bridge.

At only 32km long, the Kent is a short river but it cuts a distinct swathe through Cumbria's southern reaches and is classed as a Special Area of Conservation due to the densities of white-clawed crayfish that are found throughout much of its system, perhaps higher than anywhere else in England. Rising in the hills above Kentmere, it flows down to the estuary at Arnside, where at high spring tides the bore races upstream from Morecambe Bay. The watery perils of the estuary are well known and shouldn't be underestimated: signs warning of high tides, quicksand and hidden channels are there for good reason, and a siren is sounded before high tide, indicating that it's time for a quick retreat.

The area is the location of a number of notable sites and features. Quaint Cartmel's priory has been there since the 12th century, while the former fishing and boatbuilding villages of Grange-over-Sands and Arnside have the Victorians – and the railway – to thank for transforming them into popular holiday spots. The Lancaster Canal starts in the north of the area and, built along the natural lie of the land, offers 66km of lock-free cruising. In the south, the Arnside and Silverdale Area of Outstanding Natural Beauty (AONB) is known for its wildlife, scenery and walking. And, of course, in the centre of it all lies Morecambe Bay, a simply vast space offering unforgettable views.

View over Morecambe Bay from Fell End ▶

Cartmel to Arnside

Cartmel

Distance 10.5km **Time** 3 hours
Terrain footpaths, tracks and quiet lanes
Map OS Explorer OL7 **Access** infrequent
bus to Cartmel from Kendal

**Nestling in the wooded valley of the River
Eea on the fringe of the Lake District
National Park, attractive Cartmel is
surrounded by gentle hills offering fine
mountain and bay views.**

Start at the racecourse car park, off the
Square in Cartmel. From the far end of the
car park, walk straight on to cross the
racetrack and continue along the broad
straight track. At the fingerpost, keep
straight ahead, staying with the track as it
curves right and gently meanders uphill.

Take the left-hand fork along the tarmac
lane signed for Cark through a patchwork
of fields and stone walls. At the white
farmhouse, turn left along the footpath to
head downhill through the farmyard and
along a broad track to the road.

Crossing the road, take the footpath
uphill to initially follow the hedge, then

along the wall. Go left through the gate
and follow the wall to the lane. Taking the
driveway ahead with a fingerpost for
Templand, follow the footpath around the
back of the left-hand house and up the
narrow path by the garden, through a
small wood and across the field. Climb
over the wall steps and cross the next field
in the direction of the cottages, going
through the wide gap in the hedge and
wall and along the hedge to the lane.

Turn right into the hamlet of Templand,
then take the tarmac lane of Templand
Gate on the left, going through the gate
and down the lane. Emerging on the road,
cross this, climb over the wall and
continue along the footpath to the next
lane. Turn left here and, by the bench,
cross the wall on the right to follow the
path gently uphill, soon curving right to
rejoin the lane. Turning right, continue to
the road, cross over and keep ahead on
Grange Fell Road.

After the golf club, take the lane on the
left signed for Spring Bank Farm and just

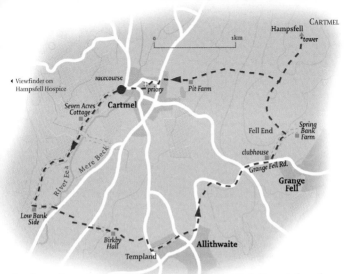

after the small pumphouse building turn left onto the footpath. Continuing ahead, pass along a shallow gully with scrubby trees out onto the open hill. The ascent is gentle and curves to follow a stone wall up to a gate (look behind for a great view). Carry on through the gate, up over the top and down the other side to a stubby waymarker at the low point (with a prominent telegraph pole off to the right).

The route back to Cartmel goes left at the waymarker, but it's worth detouring straight ahead up to the Hospice tower on Hampsfield Fell (also known as Hampsfell). Built in 1846 by the vicar of Cartmel to provide shelter, it comes complete with a little fireplace and external steps up to the roof for a fine panoramic view.

Retrace your steps to the waymarker, now heading west to follow the path downhill. Near the bottom, go through the metal kissing gate and along the wall, through the gate in the hedge and diagonally left, aiming for the right-hand side of the farm buildings.

Carry on through a couple of gates and follow the signed track back to Cartmel. Taking the path between the houses, turn left at the road and then first right along Priest Lane down to the priory. Take the footpath through the graveyard to the main entrance. The Augustinian priory, founded in 1189, partially survived the 1530s' Dissolution of the Monasteries as the villagers protested it was their parish church. The square belfry tower, constructed diagonally across the original tower, is the only one like it in the UK.

Continue out into the narrow lanes and pretty square of this enchanting village and back to the car park.

Grange-over-Sands

Distance **8.5km** Time **2 hours 30**
Terrain **pavement, footpaths, open fell**
Map **OS Explorer OL7** Access **buses to
Grange-over-Sands from Kendal and
Barrow; trains to Grange-over-Sands
from Barrow-in-Furness and Lancaster**

**Explore a holiday resort full of charm,
wander through limestone woodlands
with flowers and wildlife aplenty, and
climb Hampsfell to take in sweeping
360-degree views. The coming of the
railways was the making of this genteel
resort, soon attracting wealthy
industrialists, who built large houses
and lent the town an air of consequence.**

Turn right out of the railway station and
then left up the drive of the impressive
Netherwood Hotel. From the car park, take
the curving track off to the left, through
the waymarked gate by Brown Robin
House and through the next gate into
Cumbria Wildlife Trust's Brown Robin
Nature Reserve. This limestone
woodland is a joy to wander through at
any time of the year, noted for its spring
flowers, autumn colour and year-round
chance to spot elusive hawfinches.

Turn right at the first path up into the
woodland, following the white-topped
waymarker posts. At the path junction
near the top, turn left to wander along and
then through the large gate in the deer
fencing on the right, soon emerging from
the trees into an open field with great
views over Arnside and Milnthorpe Sands.
Continue ahead, through the gate and
then immediately left through another to
follow the track downhill. Where the
tracks meet, turn right and then quickly
left on a path down to the road.

Turning left, go around the road bend
and take the footpath signed for
Hampsfell. The path curves behind the
cottages and up into Eggerslack Wood.
Keeping ahead, cross a small stream and
bear left at the waymarker post to start
climbing. Keep heading uphill at

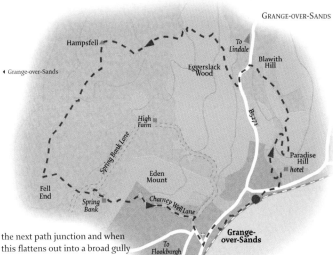

the next path junction and when this flattens out into a broad gully keep ahead on the main path. This soon curves to the left and weaves up through the woodland.

Once at the fingerpost on the woodland edge, go over the wall and climb the open limestone hillside, signed for the hospice. Cross the steps in the stone wall, turn right and continue up to the Hampsfell hospice tower, built in 1846 by the vicar of Cartmel to provide shelter. Climb the steep external steps for the panoramic view, and have a go with the compass-like toposcope.

Facing the front of the tower, take the broad grassy path heading diagonally left towards the view of Morecambe Bay. Pass a large cairn, carry on over the stone stile and head down and up the dip, keeping to the right-hand path at the fork. Fell End cairn can be seen ahead; drop down to climb over the stile and up to the cairn.

At the cairn turn sharp left, descending to pick up a grassy track which runs to the left of a copse of trees and a gully, down to a road. Cross over and take the footpath around the field, then over the drive to continue on a footpath and down the farm drive. Go around the barn, taking the waymarked footpath over the wall and uphill. Go over another stile, around the garden wall and left at the lane. Turn right at Eden Mount Close, left down Charney Well Lane and left at the sharp bend, still heading downhill.

At the T-junction, turn right, walk on past the church and at the clocktower go left onto the Main Street. Have a browse of the many interesting and independent shops along this street and at the far end turn right into the ornamental gardens. Follow the network of paths back to the railway station.

Whitbarrow

Distance 10.5km **Time** 3 hours
Terrain footpaths, open hill, quiet lanes
Map OS Explorer OL7 **Access** bus to Mill
Side from Kendal

If ever there was a walk of two halves, then this loop is it. The first half follows the foot of the scar through woodland, while the second contrasting half starts with a steep climb before returning along an exposed limestone outcrop.

Starting from the edge of Mill Side (there is parking on the roadside just across the cattle grid from the A590), head up the lane through the village. At the sharp bend, go right (signed for Beck Head only) and almost immediately, by the information panel, keep to the left fork to follow a delightful winding lane. Go over the stream at Beck Head House and continue on the lane, which becomes a public bridleway. At the fork, take the signed permitted route to the right,

through the attractive Low and High Crag Woods. This follows the foot of the Scar and offers some great views of the towering limestone crags. Cross a couple of springs and the path eventually curves to the left on approaching Witherslack Hall. The hall was built as a school from a 17th-century legacy left by Rev. John Barwick, Dean of St Paul's, and continues to this day as an independent specialist school.

Go through the gate, on past the playing field, through another gate and then through the kissing gate on the right, along a permissive path with white arrows leading through High Park Wood.

After about 1.7km, look out for an old battered waymarker post; turn right here to start the climb up the scar. It's steep in places and can be slippery. Go through the gate into the Cumbria Wildlife Trust Whitbarrow National Nature Reserve and continue up the steep gully. When the

◀ Whitbarrow Scar

path forks, take the right-hand path by the small cave to gradually climb up onto the limestone plateau. The path can be faint in places but continue ahead, aiming for the stone-built cairn known as Lord's Seat.

The reserve occupies some 100 hectares and is a patchwork of limestone pavement, low crags and scree. Wind-sculpted trees bear testimony to how exposed the site is. At first glance, it's difficult to see how anything can thrive here, but the thin soil actually provides ideal conditions for a wide variety of plants, including blue moor-grass, which is extremely rare in the UK. In summer, look out for four species of scarce fritillary butterfly, while in autumn you can spot wax cap fungi.

Having, on a clear day, enjoyed the 360-degree views, continue ahead along the top, where there's really only one obvious path to follow. After about 1km, cross the stone wall and continue ahead to the cairn. Off to the right is a fine view of Witherslack Hall. Carry on ahead as the path drops, then climbs to a cairn, before a further climb to another cairn and then an undulating stretch along the top. From the final hilltop, there are great views of the meandering River Kent, Arnside Viaduct and Morecambe Bay.

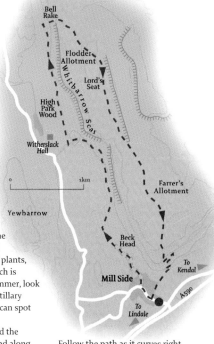

Follow the path as it curves right, heading gently downhill and soon re-entering the woodland. Following the white arrow waymarkers, go through the gate in the stone wall, bearing sharp left and back through the wall to then zigzag down the hillside; be careful as it can be muddy and slippery. At the track, turn left and then quickly right at the fingerpost, keeping on through a gate and farmyard, before arriving back at the lane in Mill Side. Turn left to return to the start.

Levens Hall Deer Park

Distance 6km **Time** 1 hour 30
Terrain footpaths, quiet lanes and
grazing fields **Map** OS Explorer OL7
Access bus to Levens Hall from Kendal

The stunning Elizabethan house seen at
Levens Hall today grew from an imposing
13th-century peel tower and sits amidst
some 9500 acres of park and agricultural
land. Laid out 300 years ago, the park and
gardens retain almost all the principal
elements of the original scheme. This
stroll takes in the river, mighty oaks,
waterfalls and some historical quirks.
Look out for the resident black fallow
deer and rare-breed Bagot goats – one of
Britain's oldest breeds.

From the lay-by just off the A6 on the
north side of Levens Bridge, cross the road
and head down to the road junction. Take
the footpath on the left just before the
river bridge and enter the Levens Hall
Estate. Follow the clearly waymarked path
as it soon rises gently above the River
Kent, passing through the undulating

parkland punctuated with stately oaks.
Leave the estate by climbing the steps in
the stone wall and turn right to follow the
wall. Carry on over the steps in the next
wall and then cross the field up to the
lane by the cottages.

Turning right, soon pass under the A590
and keep following the lane on the other
side, accompanied by the sight and sound
of the River Kent's Force Falls tumbling
below (*Force* is an old Scandinavian word
for 'waterfall'). This is also a good place
from which to watch the salmon
migration in late autumn.

At the T-junction, turn right to cross
Force Bridge – be sure to peer over at the
gushing crystal-clear waters – and
continue ahead on the footpath, passing
through the ornate metal fence signed for
Stainton and the canal towpath. The
imposing Gothic-style Sedgwick House
comes into view off to the left, complete
with its own cricket pitch. Built in 1868 it
was originally the home of the Wakefield
family, bankers and gunpowder

◄ River Kent

Sedgwick
House

Force
Bridge

Levens
Force

Back Lane

bridge

Force Lane   cottages

Lily
Wood

Wellheads
Hill

Archer's
Hill

Beech
Wood

The Avenue

A590

To
Kirkby
Lonsdale

Coppy
Wood

River Kent

0   500m

Charley
Island

Summerhouse
Hill

To
Lindale

A6

Lawrence
House
Farm

Levens
Park

Levens
Bridge

Levens
Hall

To
Milnthorpe

manufacturers, but in its time has been home to the national Fire Service and a special school under Lancashire – and not Cumbria – County Council, such has the fluidity of the county boundary been in this area.

Go through the kissing gate, over the lane and onto another footpath, climbing gently. Ahead is a lone stone bridge which looks out of place on this rural hillside. It once crossed the Lancaster Canal – started in Preston in 1792 these 'Northern Reaches' to Kendal didn't open until 1819, but it was closed to commercial traffic in 1947 with full closure in 1955.

Turning right at the bridge, follow the footpath along the fenceline until it rejoins the lane, with terrific views across the River Kent valley along the way. Going left, cross back over the A590 and, as the lane curves left, take the footpath on the right back into Levens Hall Deer Park. The first section is along a lovely avenue of old oak trees, eventually curving right to head above the river – a great vantage point for spotting wading birds such as redshank feeding on the 'beach' areas, and, if you are lucky, otters too.

Once back at the bridge, it's worth visiting Levens Hall, with its fabulous gardens, including the world's oldest topiary garden, and café, before heading back to the start.

Holme and Farleton Knott

Distance 11.5km **Time** 3 hours
Terrain country roads, field and hill
paths, scree slope, canal path
Map OS Explorer OL7 **Access** buses to
Holme from Lancaster and Keswick

Southern Cumbria is known for its
limestone pavements formed from rock
laid down in a warm, shallow sea 350
million years ago. This walk takes in one
of the finest examples, with an option to
visit another. Exposed during the ice age,
the limestone has been eroded by water
to form a pattern of cracks and crevices,
creating a distinctive geological feature.

If you want a shorter walk, there is
space for three or four cars at the point
at which you leave the lane above
Clawthorpe. From here you can either go
north to Newbiggin Crags and Farleton
Fell or south to Hutton Roof Crags.

Starting from the centre of Holme, with
The Smithy Inn on your left, head out of
the village, crossing over the canal and
the motorway. At the main road, go left
and then immediately right, following
the fingerpost for Clawthorpe. Walk
diagonally right across the parkland,
exiting by some houses. Follow the lane
ahead and, where it meets the road, go
left, uphill.

After around 500m, a fingerpost points
to the right, towards Burton. If you wish
to visit Hutton Roof Crags, head across
the field and into the wood, otherwise
continue up the lane for another 1km or
so. On reaching a gate on the left and an
information board for Hutton Roof Crags
on the right, go left through the gate and
straight ahead uphill, before veering
towards the right-hand end of Newbiggin
Crags ahead.

Where the track splits, go left and follow
it round and up onto the lower level of
the crags. Keep heading uphill and where
the path splits again, take the right fork.

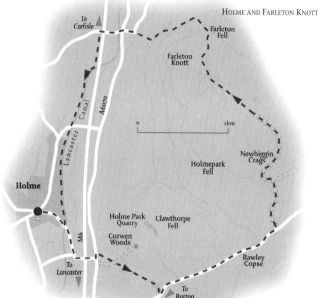

To Carlisle

Farleton Fell

Farleton Knott

Lancaster Canal

A6070

0   1km

Newbiggin Crags

Holmepark Fell

Holme

M6

Holme Park Quarry

Clawthorpe Fell

Curwen Woods

Rawley Copse

To Lancaster

To Burton

Ignoring further paths off to the right, follow the path as it bends to the left around the end of the crags. For a close-up look at the pavement, you can walk to the top of the crags – but mind your footing.

Once round the end, carry on ahead to a stile and gate, either side of a wall. Go through the gate and carry on with the wall on your left. Keep following the wall down into the dip and all the way up the other side until Farleton Knott is revealed over to the right. Make your way up to the top of the Knott and pause for the magnificent views out to Milnthorpe Sands ahead on the Kent Estuary and southwest to Morecambe Bay.

This is Open Access Land and multiple paths lead off from the top of the Knott.

Facing the estuary, leave on the path that heads off at roughly four o'clock, going downhill and bearing left every time it splits. Pass through gorse and several short steep patches of scree, then a final narrow section down to the field. At the bottom of the field, exit down the side of a house to a lane, going left here.

Emerging on the main road, go straight over and cross the bridges over the Lancaster Canal and the M6. On the far side of the motorway, take the path to the left along the edge of a field and then up some steps to reach the canal. Go right along the canal, cross over a road and continue to bridge 149. At the road, go right back into Holme.

◀ Limestone pavement

Beetham and Whin Scar

Distance 8km **Time** 2 hours 30
Terrain country roads, woodland and
field paths, farm tracks; the short stretch
across limestone pavement requires
careful footing **Map** OS Explorer OL7
Access bus to Beetham from Kendal

Waterpower has been used at Beetham
since the first mill was established here
in the 11th century, thanks to the natural
limestone weir on the River Bela. The
Heron Corn Mill is now a heritage centre.
Fell views, mythology, rare butterflies
and a fine limestone pavement sustain
interest on this route, with a café and
popular pub on hand at the end.

From the Heron Corn Mill car park in
Beetham, cross the bridge over the river
and follow the waterside path to the road,
then turn right and right again to wander
up through the village. After passing the
delightful church and Wheatsheaf Inn,
take the first road on the left, by the

village stocks, and then the path to
the right, signposted for Hale.

Walk along the backs of the houses
and then diagonally right across the
field, passing a large stone boulder
(a lone granite erratic from the Shap area)
roughly halfway. Continue to the very
top corner of the field and squeeze
through the gap in the wall.

Continue straight ahead across two
fields, pausing to admire the view of the
ruined fortified farmhouse at Beetham
Hall. At the far side of the fields, follow
the path uphill on the right, signposted
for Slackhead.

Entering the woods, keep ahead and
then take the first waymarked path on the
right. From here on, keep an eye open for
regular waymarkers, which you follow,
taking care when crossing the limestone
pavement on Whin Scar. If you're here in
August, look out for purple hairstreak
butterflies, most likely in the treetops.

◀ Beetham

On reaching a road, turn right. After passing a few houses, take the signposted path to the Fairy Steps up through the woods on the left, eventually reaching the top of the hill after a short but steep climb. Known as the Coffin Route, this was the path once used for carrying the dead from Arnside parish to consecrated ground at Beetham.

If you're feeling agile, the descent via the Fairy Steps will be a tempting challenge. If you're not, then an alternative permissive route is signposted. Local folklore has it that if you can manage the steps without touching the sides, the fairies will grant your wish.

On reaching the bottom of the steps, go right and then right again, signposted to Cockshot Lane. Ignore a path going off to the right and then, where another path joins from the right, cross this to continue diagonally left.

At Cockshot Lane, turn right along the road and then left into the woods, following the waymarked public footpath straight ahead – rather than the route signposted for Storth. At a track, go left and on reaching a lane continue straight on through the gap in the wall and across

the field, dropping down to a gate at the bottom of the hill. Cross over the road and enter the deer park (with resident deer present) to head towards the earthwork mound. On intersecting the waymarkers that run around the lower slope, go right and follow the clearly marked route over the next hill, out of the deer park and back down to the parking area at Heron Corn Mill. Finish off with refreshments at the pub and a wander around Beetham. Much of this attractive village is a conservation area.

Arnside and Blackstone Point

Distance 5.5km **Time** 2 hours
Terrain shoreline path that is impassable
during high tide – check tide times
before you leave; rocky beach, mudflats,
village road **Map** OS Explorer OL7
Access bus to Arnside from Kendal;
trains to Arnside from Lancaster and
Barrow-in-Furness

Water, walking and wildlife prove
an irresistible draw in the Arnside &
Silverdale Area of Outstanding Natural
Beauty that forms the Cumbria-
Lancashire border around the village
of Arnside. Expect crowds in summer,
but don't be deterred; the setting is
magnificent, as are the views.

This gentle walk along the shore takes
in the Kent Estuary where it opens out to
Morecambe Bay, but be aware that it's
impassable at high tide and that tides can
come in quickly. Don't be tempted to
wander out onto the mudflats.

Looking out from the waterfront
parking area in the centre of Arnside, the
51-span viaduct stretches across the Kent
Estuary. Built in 1856, it opened up access
and trade, bringing additional custom for
the local fishing and boatbuilding
industries. It was here that in around 1912
Crossfields boatyard built the *Swallow*, the
sailing dinghy immortalised by Arthur
Ransome in *Swallows and Amazons*.

From the middle of the village, head
southwest along the waterfront and at the
end of the Promenade continue down the
estuary shore in front of Ashmeadow
House. Keep going along the shore for
around 750m, skirting Grubbins Wood on
the left, and on reaching a small bay,
follow the path leftwards to reach the
access road to New Barns Caravan Park.

Go right along the road, ignoring the
road into the caravan park on the left, and
carry straight on across the grassy merse
in front of the row of houses where

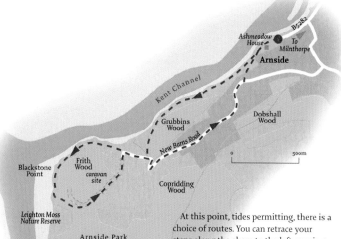

signposted for Blackstone Point 'subject to tides'. Follow the shoreline as it soon runs southwards around Frith Wood, with views opening up ahead until the vast expanse of Morecambe Bay is laid out before you at Blackstone Point. Keep to the shore around the gentle concave curve of a bay before cutting up the bank and into the woods on the left as you approach a small crag ahead.

Take the path for a short distance through the woods, ignoring paths off to the right, and on reaching the paved road that runs through the caravan park, go right. Continue along the road to emerge back at the New Barns entry point, at which go right back along the access road.

At this point, tides permitting, there is a choice of routes. You can retrace your steps along the shore to the left, passing through Grubbins Wood for some of the way if you wish. This limestone woodland nature reserve is home to a wonderful array of ferns, flowers and birds, some of which are otherwise rare in Cumbria, and offers interest at any time of year. Come in spring for bluebells, wild garlic, and greater butterfly and spotted orchids.

Alternatively, continue ahead, following the road as it bends and climbs gently to pass through the houses at the outer edge of the village. Keep ahead on New Barns Road for around 75m. Just after Parkside Drive on the right, the road drops down into a dip, at the bottom of which take the steep lane on the left between the houses towards the shore. At the bottom, go right through Beachwood Nature Reserve before dropping down to the shore and continuing back into Arnside.

◀ Arnside Promenade

Arnside Knott

Distance 10km **Time** 2 hours 30
Terrain footpaths, tracks and quiet lanes
Map OS Explorer OL7 **Access** bus to
Arnside from Kendal; trains to Arnside
from Lancaster and Barrow-in-Furness

Set at the picturesque point where
the River Kent enters Morecambe Bay,
Arnside makes an endearing start for
this scenically varied walk. From the
top of England's smallest Marilyn (hills
with a relative height of at least 150m),
Arnside Knott enjoys views to rival
those from many a higher peak.

From the far end of the promenade in
Arnside, take the waterfront path and
turn left just before the coastguard
station along the tarmac path, signed for
Knott Road/Silverdale, uphill. At the road,
turn right and, once at the sharp bend
after Parkside Drive, follow the lane off to
the left, signed for The Knott.

After passing through the gate by the
cattle grid, take the rough path of loose
stone on the left just after the first bench.

This is Open Access Land with plenty of
routes; wend your way upwards to a stone
shelter with etched panels. The limestone
hillside has a fine mosaic of habitats; look
out for rare summer butterflies, such as
high brown fritillary or scotch argus (one
of only two colonies in England).

Following the National Trust purple
arrow waymarkers, go through a kissing
gate in the wall to enter a wood and
continue ahead, soon passing a large
stone and timber bench to arrive at a
stone wall. Go sharp right here to the trig
point summit (159m), enjoying the views
over Morecambe Bay, the Kent Estuary
and the Lakeland fells.

Just after the trig point, leave the
waymarked route for the grassy path on
the left downhill – watch your step after
rain. Pass through a stand of old yews
and, at the path T-junction, turn right.
At the stone wall and fingerpost, turn
right and accompany the wall to the road.

Follow the road right, soon turning left
down the tarmac farm track with a

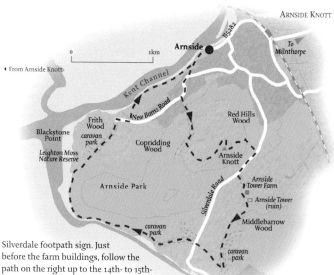

◀ From Arnside Knott

Arnside

To Milnthorpe

Kent Channel

New Barns Road

Frith Wood

Red Hills Wood

Blackstone Point

caravan park

Copridding Wood

Leighton Moss Nature Reserve

Arnside Knott

Arnside Tower Farm

Arnside Tower (ruin)

Arnside Park

Silverdale Road

Middlebarrow Wood

caravan park

caravan park

Silverdale footpath sign. Just before the farm buildings, follow the path on the right up to the 14th- to 15th-century Arnside Tower, an almost unique example of a Cumbrian peel tower. Turn right by the tower, taking the hedge-lined track to go through a kissing gate and at the caravan park take the left-hand of the two roads ahead. At the T-junction near the site entrance, go sharp right at the fingerpost, signed for Far Arnside and Arnside Knott, and into trees by the waymarker post. Continue over the fields and up to the road.

Cross over to follow the lane and carry on through the caravan park. Sticking with the waymarkers, keep to the right-hand fork at the Shore Close sign for the footpath to Arnside. This is a lovely path through woodland that hugs the coast. Once through the gate in the stone wall, take the left-hand path downhill and follow it along the top of the low cliffs

with fine views out over Morecambe Bay.

After about 1.5km, the path reaches a stone wall on the left, near another caravan park. Take the small path left going through the wall, passing a couple of benches. Look out for the narrow footpath off to the right (it can be tricky to spot), heading into the caravan park, and at the tarmac road go right (signed footpath to Arnside) to follow it out of the park to New Barns and along the edge of the estuary.

If high tide is imminent, continue along the tarmac lane, which picks up the outbound route after 1km. Otherwise, if the tide is out, go left at the fingerpost (signed Arnside via shore) to wander along the estuary and back to the start.

Index